POEMS WITH A PURPOSE FOR EVERYDAY LIFE

My Family In Christ (The World)

By Rhoda Norris

Copyright © 2021 by Rhoda Norris

Poems with a Purpose for Everyday Life

My Family in Christ (The World)

All rights reserved. No part of this publication may be reproduced, distributed, or transmitted in any form or by any means, including photocopying, recording, or other electronic or mechanical methods, without the prior written permission of the publisher, except in the case of brief quotations embodied in critical reviews and certain other noncommercial uses permitted by copyright law.

All rights reserved.

ISBN: 978-1-7373855-0-9

DEDICATION

To my Lord and Savior Jesus Christ, who is the head of my life; to my husband Michael G. Norris (a.k.a. Minister Norris G.), my partner for life.

To my grandmother Lessie B. Ellis, a beautiful, strong black woman. I miss you so much.

To my mother, Elouise Abram, I love you, ma.

To my mother-in-law, Mildred McCallum, thank you for always treating me like a daughter.

To my daughter, Shavon Dillard, I love you more than you will ever know.
To my two granddaughters, Jada and Aaliyah Dillard—no amount of words can express how much I love the both of you.

To my sisters Sylvia, Celeste, Monica, Vera, Vanessa, Torrina, and Sherry, and to my brothers Bennie, Alphonso (Dody), and Mendale—I love you all so much.

To my host of nieces and nephews—it is just too many of you to name, but you know who you are and how much you are loved by me.

To my extended family, Michael Norris Jr., Felicia Norris, and Maurice, and your wife Laura Norris, and all your children—thank you for welcoming me into the family, and much love to all of you.

And last but not least, to my very best friend Stephanie Bennet, my friend for life, and my co-workers for life at Michigan Huron Valley Women's Prison——I have so much love and respect for the officers and nurses for the work they do every day. May God continue to watch over and protect you all.
Amen!

Table of Contents

Table of Contents i
   Introduction iv

Chapter One: Trust in Jesus 2
   God Is Here 3
   Jesus Will Work It Out 4
   Every Praise 5
   Calling on Jesus Name 6
   Break Every Chain 7
   The Victory Is Mine 8
   God Is Still in Charge 9
   I Say Yes to You Lord 10
   What a Friend We Have in Jesus 11
   No Matter What Your Problem Is 12

Chapter Two: It's Time to Repent 14
   You Waited Patiently on Me 15
   Changed 16
   Open My Heart 17
   Truth Be Told 18
   War 19
   I've Been in This Storm for Far Too Long 20
   A New Life in Spite of Me 21
   I Just Wanna Be Happy 22
   God Fights for Me 23
   Through Your Grace 24

Chapter Three: Jesus – Everlasting Mercy 26
   Through It All 27
   Your Love and Favor on Me 28
   Your Word Is Good 29
   So Many Times 30
   I Never Would Have Made It 31
   Highly Favored 32
   You Delivered Me 33
   Won't God Do It? 34
   God, I Thank You 35
   You Deserve It 36

Chapter Four: The Holy Spirit Speaks..................38
I Am with You 39
Jesus Is So Real..40
Down in My Soul 41
Can't Nobody Do Me like Jesus...42
Love Theory...43
It's Working 44
Jesus I'll Never Forget 45
You Are Always Here 46
Nobody 47
The Holy Ghost 48

Chapter Five: Jesus Is Our Salvation 50
Your Church Is Still Alive 51
Amazing Grace 52
Trust in You Lord 53
Believers, Be Ready 54
Lord Help Me to Hold Out 55
God's Word Is True 56
Give This World Back to God 57
Still Able...58
Everything Is Gonna Be Alright 59
Stay on Jesus' Battlefield 60
What a Beautiful Name..61

Chapter Six: Jesus – Unstoppable Peace 63
Joy of Peace in My Soul..64
Overflow 65
God You Are So Wonderful 66
Why We Sing 67
When I Rose This Morning...68
I Lift Up My Voice..69
Soon and Very Soon 70
Since I Laid My Burdens Down 71
Sunday Mornings 72
Move on Up a Little Higher 73

Chapter Seven: God's Favor 75
I Have You in My Life Now 76
God Is My Way Maker...77
How Can This Be? 78
Lord You Hold Out Your Hand 79

Anything Can Happen 80
My Spiritual Gift 81
You Say 82
Your Love 83
Amazing 84
Because You Loved Me 85
Known 86

Chapter Eight: Working for the Lord 88
I Will Praise You in This Storm 89
You Won't Let Me Go 90
Showed Me Your Love 91
Fill Me Up 92
Your Holy Spirit 93
No Weapon 94
My God Is Awesome 95
I Woke Up With My Mind Staying on Jesus 96
I'm Not Tired Yet 97
Something about Your Wonderful Name 98

Chapter Nine: The Healing Savior 100
I Need You Now 101
Dear Lord, Have Mercy 102
Till We Meet Again 103
Jesus Promised Me a Place Over There 104
Take Me to the King 105
Jesus Promised Me a Home 106
I Can Imagine 107

Chapter Ten: The Alpha & Omega 109
Son of Heaven 110
God's Got the Whole World in His Hands 111
God's Truth and Goodness 112
Everlasting God 113
Jesus Saves 114
In the Name of Jesus 115
See You Again 116
Not Believing That Jesus Is Real 117
He's Always Right on Time 118
Lord Your Word of Truth Has Always Been Good 119
God 120

Acknowledgements 121

INTRODUCTION

Poems with a Purpose for Everyday Life, is a rare book of fiction Christian poems, that gives you scripture that is given by inspiration of God, and is profitable for doctrine, for reproof, for correction, for instruction in righteousness 2 Timothy (3 : 16).

This book of poems is for all Christians who seek God's wisdom and guidance in their everyday life, and all (The World) who have not yet found or still seek God in their everyday life. To have faith and trust in Jesus by letting him into our lives and being filled with his Holy Spirit and experiencing his kind of peace that only he can give us.

Also, knowing that our Salvation for our sins can only come through Jesus by him showing us his love and mercy and showering us with his favor—even when we are not deserving of his grace. If it is God's will, he can heal us of our sicknesses and broken-heartedness. All he wants us to do is have faith in him, confess our sins, repent of our sins, and do his good works by spreading his Good News and letting the world know that he is the one and only God. Amen

MY FAMILY IN CHRIST (THE WORLD)

Chapter One: Trust in Jesus

1. God Is Here

2. Jesus Will Work It Out

3. Every Praise

4. Calling on Jesus Name

5. Break Every Chain

6. The Victory Is Mine

7. God Is Still in Charge

8. I Say Yes to You Lord

9. What a Friend We Have in Jesus

10. No Matter What Your Problem Is

God Is Here

Even though there appears to be no hope,
You are barely hanging onto your faith and feeling spiritually broke.
Trying not to let that devil in,
But temptation is slowly taking over because you are constantly surrounded by sin.
And everywhere you turn, people are going astray,
Instead of getting closer to God, they are moving further away.
And you see all these things with your own eyes,
And even though you are barely hanging onto your own faith, you are still surprised.
How people's eyes are closed, and how they are so blind,
And you are feeling sad for them because Jesus, they are not even trying to find.
But you know deep down that he is not far away, and he is near,
And you just want people to open their eyes and see for themselves that God is here.

* * *

Sometimes it seems like there is no hope, but God will speak to you when you really need him the most. Just wait; he will speak to you when the time is right. Today, I encourage you to look up the song "God Is Here," written by Darlene Zschech. It has been sung by many people, as it is inspiring. As you listen to this song today, reflect on Isaiah 55:6-7 and think about how you may seek the Lord with all your heart. Are you seeking him today?

6 Seek ye the Lord while he may be found, call ye upon him while he is near:
7 Let the wicked forsake his way, and the unrighteous man his thoughts: and let him return unto the Lord, and he will have mercy upon him; and to our God, for he will abundantly pardon.

(Isaiah 55:6-7 KJV)

MY FAMILY IN CHRIST (THE WORLD)

Jesus Will Work It Out

When you are out there living on the street,
Wondering where you will rest your head with no food to eat.
Where is God when you need him the most?
How can you, in all of your struggles, praise him or boast?
No money in your pocket and living in despair,
Wondering where God is and wondering if he cares.
How can you put your trust in something that you cannot see?
All you can do is look up at the sky and ask, why me?
But that is when you have to trust him and let the Holy Spirit in,
Knowing that his love for you, he has not forsaken.
And try to be patient because his help is en route,
I know that it is hard for you, but continue to have faith and know—Jesus will work it out.

* * *

As much as God cares about the animals, he loves you so much more. Look up the old gospel song by Dr. Charles Hayes called "Jesus Can Work It Out" as you reflect on Matthew 6:26. Trust that he will never leave you or forsake you, and help is on the way. Won't you trust him today?

26 Behold the fowls of the air: for they sow not, neither do they reap, nor gather into barns; yet your heavenly Father feedeth them. Are ye not much better than they?
(Matthew 6:26 KJV)

Every Praise

Lord, you are the one I will look to in my time of trouble,
The one who will catch me when I fall or stumble.
Even when I cannot see my way out,
My troubles I will turn over to you because I have no doubt.
That you will be there as always to see me through,
By having faith and believing in your word, nothing can change my point of view.
Because I know that you are all that I have to lean on,
There is no one else that can get me through this life's storm.
So, my hands to heaven I will continue to raise,
Lifting them up so high and giving you every praise.

* * *

No one can get us through life's storms like Jesus! Today, listen to the song "Every Praise" by Hezekiah Walker as you reflect on Psalm 91:15 and think about how God sees us through every trouble. Do you honor God when he delivers you from your troubles?

15 He shall call upon me, and I will answer him: I will be with him in trouble; I will deliver him, and honour him.

(Psalm 91:15 KJV)

Calling on Jesus Name

When we are feeling down and out,
Jesus is the one name that we should never forget about.
Because without him, we are standing on shaky ground,
Living in a world full of sin, without God anywhere to be found.
And without him in our lives today,
Our sins just continue to pile up on us, like a stack of hay,
Until we are so buried in it that we cannot dig our way out,
Searching for God's living water but only living in a drought.
So now is the time to come to him with no feelings of shame,
Because all is forgiven by faith, repentance, and simply calling on Jesus' name.

* * *

Even though Jesus sees all your sins, he forgives you for every last one, every time, even though he paid the price for you. We are one with Christ. Today, look up the gospel song "Jesus, I Love Calling Your Name" by Shirley Caesar as you think about John 15:5, reflect on how you are one with Christ. Do you try to do things on your own? How much more blessed would your ventures be if you invited Christ's help?

5 I am the vine, ye are the branches: He that abideth in me, and I in him, the same bringeth forth much fruit: for without me ye can do nothing.

(John 15:5 KJV)

MY FAMILY IN CHRIST (THE WORLD)

Break Every Chain

When you are weighted down because of your sin,
And all you have is your guilt feelings, lying so heavy within.
Trying so hard to do all things on your own to make it right,
But you keep falling deeper into sin because, without God, you have no hope in sight.
So, you still keep trying to fight your way through your own temptations,
Not knowing with God's help, he has no limitations.
And with him by your side, his help will always remain,
He is just standing there waiting to forgive you and break every chain.

* * *

This poem was inspired by the song "Break Every Chain," performed by Tasha Cobbs. Today, listen to this song and think about the ability to break every chain through the power of Jesus as you reflect on Ephesians 1:7. Only Jesus has the power to forgive us of our sins, granting us sweet freedom. Have you asked him for your forgiveness?

7 In whom we have redemption through his blood, the forgiveness of sins, according to the riches of his grace.

(Ephesians 1:7 KJV)

The Victory Is Mine

Yes, family, when you can't seem to resist temptation and do what is right,
Even in your darkest moments, God will never leave your sight.
He will always be right there to see you through,
Just keep having faith in him; that is all he wants you to do.
And know, that for you, he will be there; and you have to just hold on,
Because his love and mercy for the faithful is forever—and will never be withdrawn.
So, keep the faith even in your temptations and let God be your stronghold,
Because his presence in your life is more precious than money, wealth, and even gold.
Because only God can give you the fruit of his strength to eat off his vine,
He will give you the kind of courage to face your temptations and say, "Devil! The victory is all mine."

* * *

Amen! The victory is yours and the victory is mine! Praise God we have victory through Jesus' sacrifice. Through Jesus, we can claim victory in Jesus' name. Today, as you reflect on this poem and Ephesians 6:10-11, look up the old hymn "Victory Is Mine" and worship Jesus as you claim victory over Satan today!

10 Finally, my brethren, be strong in the Lord, and in the power of his might.
11 Put on the whole armour of God, that ye may be able to stand against the wiles of the devil.

(Ephesians 6:10-11 KJV)

God Is Still in Charge

Yes, family, God is always there for you and me,
We just have to stand firm in our faith and believe.
That there is nothing that our Lord and Savior, Jesus Christ, can't do,
No matter what it is, family, he will always see us through.
Because he said, ask, and it shall be given,
God wants us to live by his word and have faith in him; that is how we should be livin'.
And as long as we are obedient to him, it was always agreed,
That he would take care of our every need.
So, remember, my family—no matter if the problem is small or large,
God has the final say, and he is the one who is still in charge.

* * *

No matter what Satan thinks, our God is still in charge! Today, look up the song "God Is Still in Charge" by Willie Banks and the Messengers as you reflect on John 6:35. There is nothing that Jesus cannot do, and he will fulfill your every need if you just come to him. What needs do you have today?

35 And Jesus said unto them, I am the bread of life: he that cometh to me shall never hunger; and he that believeth on me shall never thirst.

(John 6:35 KJV)

MY FAMILY IN CHRIST (THE WORLD)

I Say Yes to You Lord

Lord, you are the only one that I can call on,
Because in my times of trouble, only you can make my troubles be gone.
So, I will continue to look to you for everything,
Because I know the truth is what your word will always bring.
So, I will live for your truth, dear Lord, and on your word I will only rely,
Because the world chooses to live not in truth—but a lie.
But I know how great you and your word truly are,
How your loving mercy reaches everywhere, no matter how far.
So, for you, I will always be right here, ready to serve,
Because my undying commitment to you, dear Jesus, is what you deserve.
And by me, you will always be loved and adored,
And whatever work you need from me—I say yes, to you, Lord.

* * *

How wonderful it is to just say, "Yes," to the Lord! Today, as you reflect on this poem and Proverbs 16:3, commit all your works to the Lord and all your thoughts and feelings to Jesus. Are you still holding back today? Look up the gospel song "I'll Say Yes to My Lord," by Nate Bean & 4Given, featuring Lady Adrian Lewis-Freeman. It's a great version to get you excited about the Lord today! Just say, "Yes," to the Lord.

3 Commit thy works unto the Lord, and thy thoughts shall be established.

(Proverbs 16:3 KJV)

What a Friend We Have in Jesus

My God, we always come to you,
When we have troubles that we can't seem to get through.
But we know that no matter how bad it may be,
You told us that you are a forgiving God and that you "would not forsake thee."
As long as we come to you with an open heart and mind,
Your love and mercy for us, we would always find.
And our sins you will always forgive,
But we have to change our hearts and the way we live.
Because you said we are your people and you will always be there for us,
So, we will know without a doubt that we have a friend in you, dear Jesus.

* * *

What a comforting thought to know without a doubt, we have a friend in Jesus. So, today, look up the old hymn "What a Friend We Have in Jesus" and find the version by Aretha Franklin, who does a wonderful rendition of this song, and I encourage you to and listen to it as you reflect on 1 Samuel 12:22. The Lord will never forsake his people for any reason, because he is very pleased to have you in his presence! Do you delight in the Lord's presence today?

22 For the Lord will not forsake his people for his great name's sake: because it hath pleased the Lord to make you his people.

(1 Samuel 12:22 KJV)

No Matter What Your Problem Is

God has a way of working your problems out,
He will never forsake you or leave you without.
He wants you to depend on him in your time of need,
Don't ever think that he doesn't hear your cries or pleas.
Just keep praying and having faith in him,
Even when things seem impossible and grim.
Just believe that he will not let you fall,
Sometimes you just have to have that strong, bold faith, that's all.
And know that Jesus loves you and he considers you his,
He will always be there for you, no matter what your problem is.

* * *

How many times have you been asked how you're doing, and you just say, "Fine," because you figure no one wants to hear how you really are? Jesus wants to hear it, every time. He never tires of hearing about your worries or fears; he wants us to lay all our troubles at his feet. No matter how impossible or dire the situation may seem, today, listen to the song "Wait" by Marvin Sapp as you reflect on 1 Peter 5:7, and remember, Jesus will always work it out. Will you trust him?

7 Casting all your care upon him; for he careth for you.

(1 Peter 5:7 KJV)

MY FAMILY IN CHRIST (THE WORLD)

Chapter Two: It's Time to Repent

1. You Waited Patiently on Me
2. Changed
3. Open My Heart
4. Truth Be Told
5. War
6. I've Been in This Storm for Far Too Long
7. A New Life in Spite of Me
8. I Just Wanna Be Happy
9. God Fights for Me
10. Through Your Grace

You Waited Patiently on Me

I have been walking through life without you for such a long time,
I never thought I needed you, dear Jesus; it never crossed my mind.
I was so use to doing everything on my own,
But now I realize that without you, God, my life has been so empty and alone.
And I always thought that I had everything I ever needed,
Not knowing that without you in my life, the tasks you have for me could never be completed.
And finally, I am opening my eyes for the first time and seeing so clear,
How I was living in a world of darkness, but for me, you were always here.
And even though I was so blind to my sins that I could not see,
That you were always standing there, dear Jesus, waiting patiently on me.

* * *

The Lord is so good he gives us time to come to him. Not many of us have that kind of patience. Today, as you reflect on Proverbs 28:26, know that it's better to trust the Lord to find wisdom. Look up the song "You Waited" by Travis Greene and as you listen to it, think about how amazing it is that God waited so patiently for each one of us. We, too, should have more patience with others. Will you pray for patience today?

26 He that trusteth in his own heart is a fool: but whoso walketh wisely, he shall be delivered.

(Proverbs 28:26 KJV)

Changed

I have always sought you with half a heart,
Trying to read your word in the middle of the Bible instead of learning your word from the start.
And not trying to understand about you and what I had read,
Thinking I knew all about you, from what other people said.
Even though I did not know what they were telling me was true,
Because I did not take the time out for myself, dear Jesus, to learn about you.
Because I thought all I needed was in you, was to believe,
But I realize now to know you, that I have to study and read.
And, even though I always thought that you were so close, I realize now that from me, you were so far,
I never really knew you, Lord; I really don't know who you are.
So, now on my own, I study your word and my life had to be rearranged,
After I found out about your love and sacrifice for me, my life has been changed.

* * *

It's never wise to assume anything about God, even if someone else tells you it's true! We were given the Bible, so that we could do our own research. When you pass on information that isn't true, just because you didn't research it, you become a fool. Has this ever happened to you? Today, look up the gospel song "Changed" by Tramaine Hawkins and listen to it. As you reflect on this poem and Romans 1:21-22, commit to researching all things in the Bible for yourself.

21 Because that, when they knew God, they glorified him not as God, neither were thankful; but became vain in their imaginations, and their foolish heart was darkened. 22 Professing themselves to be wise, they became fools.

(Romans 1:21-22 KJV)

Open My Heart

Dear Lord, my life has been one big race,
Thinking that I was going somewhere and ending up no place.
I did not feel like I needed you where I was going,
Just the mention of your name to me was so annoying.
Because God-fearing people kept telling me that I needed to take you with me wherever I go,
But I did not want to hear it because, with my life, I was running the show.
As far as I was concerned, I did not need you in my life,
Because I did not know that I was slowly killing my soul with the devil's knife.
And even though I heard a voice deep inside,
Telling me to repent and calling me to stand by your side.
I ignored the voice and continued to live in my sins because I thought I was smart,
But now, dear Jesus, I cannot hear that voice anymore; and to you, I don't know how to open my heart.

* * *

Before we truly know the love of Jesus and have him in our hearts, we often run in the other direction until we're weary, not realizing how hard we're fighting against him. Today, listen to the song "Open My Heart" by Yolanda Adams as you reflect on Deuteronomy 28:47-48. Do you need to open your heart to Christ?

47 Because thou servedst not the Lord thy God with joyfulness, and with gladness of heart, for the abundance of all things;
48 Therefore shalt thou serve thine enemies which the Lord shall send against thee, in hunger, and in thirst, and in nakedness, and in want of all things: and he shall put a yoke of iron upon thy neck, until he have destroyed thee.

(Deuteronomy 28:47-48 KJV)

Truth Be Told

Lord, sometimes I live my life on a lie,
Trying to put my best self for the world to see, and I don't know why.
I feel that I have to be something that I am not,
Thinking that this life I have on this earth right now is all that I've got.
Not giving a thought to you or your word,
Not caring about all of your suffering on the cross for me that occurred.
But trying to hold onto the material things of this world that I continue to chase after,
Not caring that these things are leading my salvation and soul into disaster.
So, in my life, I keep playing this dangerous game,
Not thinking that my time is gonna run out, and right now, there is no need for me to change.
But I know without you, God, that I am living my life full of chances that are so bold,
I am living my life for Satan right now—if the truth be told.

* * *

It's a scary thought knowing that we're being stalked continuously. But that's the way of it. The devil continuously stalks each one of us in hopes of leading us astray from our Lord and Savior. He wants to ruin our testimony in front of as many people as possible, so that he may keep as many people from Christ as possible. What a terrible goal. That's why we must keep Christ at the forefront of our minds. Today, as you reflect on 1 Peter 5:8, look up the song "Truth Be Told" by Matthew West, and ask yourself if you've really been honest with yourself. When others look at you, would they say you are living for Christ or Satan today?

8 Be sober, be vigilant; because your adversary the devil, as a roaring lion, walketh about, seeking whom he may devour.

(1 Peter 5:8 KJV)

MY FAMILY IN CHRIST (THE WORLD)

War

The devil is always trying to jump at a chance to steal your peace,
That is why you have to stay prayed up at all times, so that your faith in God will increase.
Because the devil, if he can, your heart and mind he will attack,
And once that happens, it will be so hard to get your faith in the Lord back.
So, at all times, you must be aware and alert,
Because the devil's evil plans, he will always try to insert.
Through your heart, mind, body, and soul,
And once that happens, he will be in total control.
So, to your temptations, you cannot give in,
Because you don't want your soul to be lost; you don't want that devil to win.
So, the devil is not what you want to play with, or look for,
Because once you let him in, your soul's struggle of right and wrong will be at war.

* * *

It's usually only after we've done something wrong that we realize just how wrong it was, during the aftermath. If we're blessed enough, these mistakes occur during childhood, and a good parental figure will punish us harshly enough that we won't forget the consequences of our poor choices. God is a good father—the best father. He punishes us for our wrongdoing and poor choices so that we may live life abundantly and happily, at peace. He doesn't want to see us struggling in sin with our souls at war. Today, listen to the song "War" by Charles Jenkins & Fellowship Chicago as you reflect on Ephesians 6:10-12. Stay strong in the Lord, clothed in the whole armor of God in prayer. Are you at war within yourself today? Pray.

10 Finally, my brethren, be strong in the Lord, and in the power of his might.
11 Put on the whole armour of God, that ye may be able to stand against the wiles of the devil.
12 For we wrestle not against flesh and blood, but against principalities, against powers, against the rulers of the darkness of this world, against spiritual wickedness in high places.
(Ephesians 6:10-12 KJV)

MY FAMILY IN CHRIST (THE WORLD)

I've Been in This Storm for Far Too Long

I feel like my life has been one big swirl,
Going around in circles, thinking that I had all the time in the world.
Putting all my time in the here and now,
Living my life to the fullest was my only vow.
Not caring how much I lived in my sins,
Doing whatever I wanted to do was how my days would always begin.
Living for today and not caring about tomorrow,
Your words of Salvation, dear Jesus, I did not follow.
Instead, I was living my life in ruins and confusion,
Finally realizing that turning my life over to you, God, was my only conclusion.
So, God, I can only pray that your love and mercy, for me, you will prolong,
Because I have been living in this storm for far too long.

* * *

If you feel like your life has been under fire for a long time, many of us have been in some very long storms of our own, too. Look up the old gospel song "I've Been in This Storm for Far Too Long" by Mighty Clouds of Joy and listen to it as you reflect on Romans 6:23. What a blessing to find relief from the storms of this life in everlasting life through Jesus Christ our Lord. Have you thanked him for his mercy today?

23 For the wages of sin is death; but the gift of God is eternal life through Jesus Christ our Lord.

(Romans 6:23 KJV)

A New Life in Spite of Me

God has been there with me through thick and thin,
Even when I did not want to follow him, and I kept living in sin.
I just wanted to continue to do all things on my own,
But God kept holding on to me because, in my life, his seed was already sown.
Even though I was living in a world full of conflict and strife,
I did not realize that his plans were always in the making for my life.
To give me peace and allow me to rest,
He showed me how not living for him my life was under so much stress.
So, I thank you, Lord, because you gave me peace of mind and opened my eyes to see,
A wonderful new life to live, in spite of me.

* * *

God still finds a way to pave a pathway to a wonderful new life for us, despite our mistakes and sins. Today, as you reflect on 1 Peter 4:2, listen to Tasha Cobbs' song "In Spite of Me" and think of how the Lord must love us so much to continue working in our lives despite our sinful nature. We should be so grateful for his mercy and love. Are you doing the will of God?

2 That he no longer should live the rest of his time in the flesh to the lusts of men, but to the will of God.

(1 Peter 4:2 KJV)

MY FAMILY IN CHRIST (THE WORLD)

I Just Wanna Be Happy

Dear Lord, I do not know why I keep making the same mistakes,
I keep taking the same road into sin; I need a different route to take.
Help lead me onto the right path,
Help me to do your good works on your behalf.
Let everything I am, shine like your light,
Let everyone see, in me, your joy and delight.
Because I know that you, Lord, are my strength and tower,
You are the one I will come running to because, in this world, you hold all the power.
And I know that nothing can be done without your mighty hand,
Because you created everything in this world, and I know that you are the great I Am.
So, to you, I will always praise and worship gladly,
Because I want to live for you, dear Jesus; I just wanna be happy.

* * *

    Don't we all just want to be happy? Today, look up the song "Wanna Be Happy" by Kirk Franklin and listen to it as you reflect on Proverbs 4:11-13. Jesus knows how you feel, even though you seem to keep taking the same roads into sin. Keep trying because, with practice, we make better habits in life. It gets easier to rely on Jesus when you make it a habit. What strongholds do you need God's strength in your life for today? Just ask.

11 I have taught thee in the way of wisdom; I have led thee in right paths.
12 When thou goest, thy steps shall not be straitened; and when thou runnest, thou shalt not stumble.
13 Take fast hold of instruction; let her not go: keep her; for she is thy life.
(Proverbs 4:11-13 KJV)

God Fights for Me

I know, Lord, that I am not perfect, and I can do wrong,
I am sometimes weak in my temptation, and I can't find the strength to be strong.
Sometimes it is hard for me to hold on to my faith,
It is a continued battle with Satan, and my soul he's trying to take.
And I keep running and running with no place to hide,
Thinking that I can do battle on my own without you, dear Lord, being my guide.
But every time I go it alone, I stumble and fall,
Because I did not bother to call on you, my God, no, not at all.
Now I realized that without you, my battle is lost, and I must agree,
That I need you here always, God, to fight for me.

* * *

Satan tries really hard to make us forget that God is always in our corner. Today, as you reflect on James 4:7, listen to Charity Gayle's song, "God Fights for Me." Satan has already lost the battle; just remember to resist him, and he will flee. Are you struggling today?

7 Submit yourselves therefore to God. Resist the devil, and he will flee from you.
(James 4:7 KJV)

MY FAMILY IN CHRIST (THE WORLD)

Through Your Grace

I always believed with hard work, I could accomplish anything,
Not realizing without you, dear Lord, I actually have nothing.
Only you can give me the true fruit of my labors,
By following your word to love and help my neighbors.
And that means I must sometimes make a sacrifice,
To help someone in need that I don't even know by showing love and kindness or just being nice.
And always willing to help the sick and poor,
Willing to put my trust in you, dear Lord, to open the most impossible doors.
And I know whatever you have planned, no one can stop,
No matter how they try, you will always have the victory and come out on top.
Even though I know there will be my own troubles that I'm going to face,
I know that I will come through it by your grace.

* * *

Everything we own belongs to God, and it's by his grace he gives us all we have. He is our father in heaven, and much like our own parents (if they are good parents), he wants to bless us here on earth while we are here. He doesn't want to see us go through hardships and trials, but we do have to go through them to learn from them. Today, look up the song "God's Grace" performed by Trin-i-tee 5:7 and listen to it as you reflect on this poem and Colossians 3:12. Consider what you're doing in your life. Are you humbly helping others?

12 Put on therefore, as the elect of God, holy and beloved, bowels of mercies, kindness, humbleness of mind, meekness, longsuffering.

(Colossians 3:12 KJV)

MY FAMILY IN CHRIST (THE WORLD)

Chapter Three: Jesus – Everlasting Mercy

1. Through It All

2. Your Love and Favor on Me

3. Your Word Is Good

4. So Many Times

5. I Never Would Have Made It

6. Highly Favored

7. You Delivered Me

8. Won't God Do It?

9. God, I Thank You

10. You Deserve It

MY FAMILY IN CHRIST (THE WORLD)

Through It All

Dear Lord, it took me so long to get here,
I was so busy for a long time chasing after money and my career.
I did not have enough time for you, to seek,
I did not even have enough time to pray, or about you, to think.
I just went on living my life for me,
I was so blind to worldly possessions, and those things were all I could see.
I did not know that without you, my life was just a big waste,
I was willing to run after every material thing I wanted, but you, I was not willing to chase.
And even though I was not deserving, to me, you still took hold,
I realize now that you not only show mercy to the good, but the foolish and to the old.
So, for whatever reason, dear Lord, you chose me to call,
And even though it took me a long time to come to you, God, you stuck with me through it all.

* * *

Today, as you reflect on this poem and Matthew 13:22, consider how forgiving the Lord is to love us through everything. The song "Through It All" was written by the gifted musician Andrae Crouch many years ago but still rings true today. Consider listening to this song and thanking God for loving you, through it all.

22 He also that received seed among the thorns is he that heareth the word; and the care of this world, and the deceitfulness of riches, choke the word, and he becometh unfruitful.
(Matthew 13:22 KJV)

MY FAMILY IN CHRIST (THE WORLD)

Your Love and Favor on Me

I never thought I had the protection of your shield,
Because I was not willing to pray and fall down on my knees and kneel.
But you still said that my soul you wanted to save,
Even though my time and prayer to you, I never gave.
And you never held it against me; I was still your child,
Even when I was living in my sins and living my life so wild.
There was still something about me that you thought was special,
You were determined to use your Holy Spirit inside of me as a vessel.
By spreading your good news to all people and not caring about race,
Showing your love and mercy to all mankind through your good grace.
So, I thank you, God, for setting my soul free,
By your Holy Spirit and showing all your love and favor on me.

* * *

It's only through the Holy Spirit inside of us that we can react to hateful people with love. Often, it's the devil being hateful to us, not the people themselves. We must love the people who are oppressed by Satan, for it's the only way to reach them with God's love. We must allow the Holy Spirit to do God's work, through us, the vessel that carries the spirit. Today, as you reflect on this poem and Psalm 32:7, listen to Hezekiah Walker's song "God Favored Me," and praise the Lord, for he shows favor on us all, no matter our race or creed. He created each one of us, and we are all so beautiful to him. Won't you love your brothers and sisters in Christ?

7 Thou art my hiding place; thou shalt preserve me from trouble; thou shalt compass me about with songs of deliverance. Selah.

(Psalm 32:7 KJV)

Your Word Is Good

Lord, how much I praise and worship you,
Thinking for a long time that I was unworthy, living a life that was untrue.
Feeling like I could not measure up to your mercy and kindness,
Because I was living a life of confusion and blindness.
But you showed me how to live my life right,
You brought me out of my darkness into your wonderful light.
So now I know that you are the only one who can seat me in a high place,
And I know this to be true, deep in my soul, even though I have never seen your face.
And now all I want is to get close to you as I can,
By spreading your good news to every child, woman, and man.
And by letting them know that your word of truth has always stood,
Through the ends of time—your word is good.

* * *

Only God can bring us out of the darkest depths of the world into the light of peace. So many people have risen from the worst situations by the grace of God. Today, look up the song "You Are Good" by Israel Houghton and listen to it as you think about your situation. As you reflect on 1 John 3:1, ask yourself what you truly desire in life. Do your desires align with God's desires or worldly desires? Commit to becoming closer to God today.

1 Behold, what manner of love the Father hath bestowed upon us, that we should be called the sons of God: therefore the world knoweth us not, because it knew him not.

(1 John 3:1 KJV)

MY FAMILY IN CHRIST (THE WORLD)

So Many Times

Lord, when I could not find my way back to you,
So lost in my sins, I did not know what to do.
Feeling so lost and from you; astray,
No strength to carry on, unable to find my way.
But you picked me up and led me on the right road,
Filling me with your Holy Spirit, which was always foretold.
That all I had to do was have faith and believe,
And allow the Holy Spirit into my life to always lead.
Because I know that your love and mercy is one of a kind,
That same love and mercy you have shown to me, through my sins, so many times.

* * *

No matter how far you wander off on the wrong path, it only takes one step to head back in the right direction. Sin has a way of being gradual. You take one little step into sin, then another and another, and before you know it, you're in deep—over-your-head deep. And if you don't see a way out, you have to submit yourself before the Lord and do the right thing, whatever it may be. God will meet you there. Today, look up the gospel song "So Many Times the Lord Made a Way for Me" by Debra Snipes and the Angels, and listen to it as you reflect on this poem and Isaiah 55:7. Will you turn from your sin today?

7 Let the wicked forsake his way, and the unrighteous man his thoughts: and let him return unto the LORD, and he will have mercy upon him; and to our God, for he will abundantly pardon.

(Isaiah 55:7 KJV)

I Never Would Have Made It

I look at my life, where I did not have any hope,
Not knowing you, dear Lord, and not having any other way to cope.
Living a life trying to make it with no plan,
I did not realize that all I needed was your helping hand.
So, I had to go through life with a lesson learned,
Not the people of this world, but your love and mercy are what I needed to earn.
So, I had to change my life and how I had thought,
By reading your word is the only way I could be taught.
And to see for myself what others were talking about,
And now that I have learned all about you, dear Jesus, your name is all I want to shout.
And how good it feels to spread your good news and your love, I must admit,
That without you, dear Jesus, I never would have made it.

* * *

If you have ever thought you weren't going to make it through, just know we've all been in your shoes. Without Jesus, life is so much harder. Today, listen to the song "I Never Would Have Made It" by Marvin Sapp and reflect on 2 Peter 3:18. Staying in God's word is the only way we can learn and grow in his knowledge and grace. Are you reading your Bible daily?

18 But grow in grace, and in the knowledge of our Lord and Saviour Jesus Christ. To him be glory both now and for ever. Amen.

(2 Peter 3:18 KJV)

MY FAMILY IN CHRIST (THE WORLD)

Highly Favored

Lord, you brought me through some mighty hard times,
I remember being hungry—no food to eat, no money, not even a dime.
I did not have a place to lay my head,
Wondering some days if I was better off dead.
Not being able to see my way through the hunger and pain,
Not wanting to feel the empty hunger in my stomach, over and over again.
But even through all of this, you did not let me suffer long,
It only made me closer to you, and my suffering was never prolonged.
And I never gave up hope because I knew that I was all yours,
And I knew the key to my success was going to be through your open doors.
So, I kept going, and you made sure that I had enough to sustain,
Even when I did not see it, you make sure all my needs were still obtained.
So, Lord, I abound in all your mercy and grace, and every moment I savor,
And I thank you, dear Jesus, for all things that I have gone through, and I know by you that I am still blessed and highly favored.

* * *

This poem was inspired by the song "Blessed and Highly Favored" by The Clark Sisters. Sometimes, we go through some major trials, but that does not mean God has forsaken us! God's grace is always sufficient. Today, take a listen to the song as you reflect on 2 Corinthians 12:9 and think about the power of Christ. What major trial has he brought you through?

9 And he said unto me, My grace is sufficient for thee: for my strength is made perfect in weakness. Most gladly therefore will I rather glory in my infirmities, that the power of Christ may rest upon me.

(2 Corinthians 12:9 KJV)

You Delivered Me

My Lord, there are so many things that I have been through,
And love and kindness in my life, I had never known before you.
I always felt like I was born in this world all alone,
Never really having anything or anyone that I can truly call my own.
Faking as I was going along in life and hoping that no one would call my bluff,
Always having a feeling so deep inside of me saying that I was not good enough.
So, I would smile and laugh, and all my insecurities I would hide,
Only showing the person who was smiling and laughing on the outside.
But on the inside, I was always searching for someone to hold onto,
Searching for someone in this world instead of searching for you.
But you came along, dear Lord, and set all my insecurities free,
By showing your love and mercy, you delivered me.

* * *

Many of us feel like we don't fit in—somewhere. Be it in school, or family, or work. Some social setting, at some point, we feel like a social outcast. Jesus chose 12 disciples who were all social outcasts to be his followers. He didn't go up into the synagogues and pick the great leaders for his chosen few; no, he chose the broken and unloved. Jesus loves us all, and he looks at the heart. God knitted you together in your mother's womb, and as Psalm 139:13-14 says, you were fearfully and wonderfully made, and everything about you was put together exactly how God wanted you to be. You are meant to be exactly how you are. Today, listen to the song "Deliver Me" (This Is My Exodus featuring Le'Andria Johnson) by Donald Lawrence & the Tri-City Singers as you reflect on this poem. God loves you, just the way you are. Can you let your insecurities go and be secure in God's love today?

13 For thou hast possessed my reins: thou hast covered me in my mother's womb.
14 I will praise thee; for I am fearfully and wonderfully made: marvellous are thy works; and that my soul knoweth right well.

(Psalm 139:13-14 KJV)

MY FAMILY IN CHRIST (THE WORLD)

Won't God Do It?

Even though all around me I see this world falling apart,
I know that you will never leave me, dear Lord, because I feel it so deep in my heart.
I feel your mighty shield surrounding me to protect,
And in my times of trouble, I will lean on you, and your mighty powers I will never disrespect.
Because I know that there is nothing that you cannot do,
Dear Jesus, you have a multitude of followers even though you started out with only a few.
Filling us all with your wonderful Holy Spirit and joy,
A gift for anyone who wants to accept it and enjoy.
Because your love for me is like a breath of fresh air,
I can search all over for a love like yours, and no other can compare.
A love that grows stronger bit by bit,
I just want to shout to the world, if you have faith, won't God do it?

* * *

When our hearts are in the right place, and our faith is strong, God will provide. Today, as you reflect on this poem and Ephesians 6:10, ask yourself if you doubt the power of God. Look up the gospel song "Won't He Do It" by Koryn Hawthorne and listen to it. Do you trust God in all things, at all times? He can do all things; be strong in the Lord today, family.

10 Finally, my brethren, be strong in the Lord, and in the power of his might.
(Ephesians 6:10 KJV)

God, I Thank You

Dear Lord, all through the years,
I've had to shed a lot of tears.
But that never stopped me from keeping my faith in you,
Because for me, you were always there, I always knew.
There was never any doubt in my mind,
That you would always pick me up and never leave me behind.
Because you said to keep having faith and believing in you,
So, I never gave up spreading your good news, if only to a few.
Telling anyone who would listen to what I had to say,
That you, dear Lord, did not let any obstacles stand in my way.
So, God, I want to give you all the praise and honor for all that you do,
Because I can never say how much, God, I thank you.

* * *

Every time we come through a trial, it grows our faith. For those who have witnessed God's grace through each trial, we can't thank him enough for his mercy and grace. Today, listen to the worship song "Thank You, Lord" by Don Moen as you reflect on this poem and 1 Peter 1:6-7. Think about your relationship with God. Have you thanked God today?

6 Wherein ye greatly rejoice, though now for a season, if need be, ye are in heaviness through manifold temptations:
7 That the trial of your faith, being much more precious than of gold that perisheth, though it be tried with fire, might be found unto praise and honour and glory at the appearing of Jesus Christ.

(1 Peter 1:6-7 KJV)

You Deserve It

Thank you, Lord, for being there when I was afraid and worried,
I prayed to you, my God, and peace within me came in a hurry.
I was very lost and confused,
But the power of your prayer I did use.
Because it made me see that through my prayers and faith, I am strong,
A child of the most high is to whom I belong.
So now, I will never forget when trouble comes my way,
To get down on my knees and to you, I will always pray.
And spreading your good news, dear Jesus, I'm never going to quit,
Always giving you the praise and honor because you deserve it.

* * *

    Only Jesus deserves our praise. It's nice to hear praises when we do good, but it's only through Jesus we have the example of what good works are. When we follow Christ's examples, we, too, do good works. As you reflect on this poem and 1 Thessalonians 5:16-18, ask yourself if you rejoice and pray every day. Do you pray when trouble comes your way? Jesus did. The Bible often talked of Jesus going off by himself to talk to the Father when he was troubled. Today, look up the song "You Deserve It" by JJ. Hairston and worship the Lord.

16 Rejoice evermore.
17 Pray without ceasing.
18 In every thing give thanks: for this is the will of God in Christ Jesus concerning you.
                                                              (1 Thessalonians 5:16-18 KJV)

MY FAMILY IN CHRIST (THE WORLD)

MY FAMILY IN CHRIST (THE WORLD)

Chapter Four: The Holy Spirit Speaks

1. I Am With You

2. Jesus Is So Real

3. Down in My Soul

4. Can't Nobody Do Me Like Jesus

5. Love Theory

6. It's Working

7. Jesus I'll Never Forget

8. You Are Always Here

9. Nobody

10. The Holy Ghost

I Am With You

How do I move when something seems so big?
When I can't find the courage to move, dear Lord, and your words, from me, seem hid.
And I search for your words of encouragement so that I can move,
But all of this doubt that I am feeling, I can't seem to remove.
And because of this doubt, I am stuck in one place,
Why do I seem to forget that your words are what I need to embrace?
To get me through all the things I need to conquer,
Why do I not move, dear Lord? Why do I sit around and ponder?
Why am I thinking so hard about a plan?
When I already know that you have my future in your hands.
So, now I must move, and I know this to be true,
By reading and believing in your scripture that says, go, because I am with you.

* * *

No matter what you're going through, God is with you through it all. Through all your struggles and all your pain, no matter what it is, he is there. When you stay in God's word every day, you have that constant, comforting reminder. Today, listen to the Maranatha! Singers, "I Will Be With You" as you reflect on Joshua 1:9, and remind yourself to be strong, keep the faith. Are you struggling today? He is with you.

9 Have not I commanded thee? Be strong and of a good courage; be not afraid, neither be thou dismayed: for the Lord thy God is with thee whithersoever thou goest.

(Joshua 1:9 KJV)

MY FAMILY IN CHRIST (THE WORLD)

Jesus Is So Real

There is something inside of me that speaks to me every day,
Especially when I'm doing wrong, the guilt feelings never go away.
A voice that tells me to do what is right, from deep within,
A voice that warns me to stay away from sin.
A voice that tells me even when things go wrong to keep having faith,
A voice that tells me to pray and not to hesitate.
A voice that warns me to stay away from danger,
That same voice of Jesus, who saved me from my sins, who was born in a manger.
So, I know that the Holy Spirit is what I feel,
The one who lives inside of me is you, dear Jesus, who is so real.

* * *

All God's people should feel guilty when they're doing wrong or feel a pull to do the right thing. That's how you know you truly have the Holy Spirit within you. It's the voice of truth, from the Spirit of truth, as described in John 14:16-17. As you reflect on these verses today, look up "Jesus Is Real" by The New Life Community Choir (featuring John P. Kee) and ask yourself if you feel this pull. Do you heed the call and obey God's commands through his Spirit of truth?

16 And I will pray the Father, and he shall give you another Comforter, that he may abide with you for ever;
17 Even the Spirit of truth; whom the world cannot receive, because it seeth him not, neither knoweth him: but ye know him; for he dwelleth with you, and shall be in you.
(John 14:16-17 KJV)

Down in My Soul

God, there is something so deep in my spirit that I am feeling,
Something that is working inside of me like a spiritual healing.
Something that is cleansing me deep inside,
Wanting to confess my sins to you, dear Lord, that I no longer want to hide.
So, to you, I come ashamed and broken,
Confessing the things I have done that have never been spoken.
And now I am coming to you with everything on the line,
I don't want my sins to be how my life will be defined.
So, Lord, I am asking you to forgive me of my sins,
Because now living and spreading your good news is how I want my life to end.
And living by your word brings eternal life I was told,
And I know it to be true, by the Holy Spirit telling me—deep down in my soul.

* * *

There's something so cleansing about baring our souls before the Lord when we confess our sins and leave them at the feet of Jesus. The freedom of letting all that weight go is so uplifting. Today, listen to "Down in My Soul" by The Ingram Gospel Singers as you reflect on this poem and Ephesians 3:16-17. Consider any sins in your life. What do you need to confess today?

16 That he would grant you, according to the riches of his glory, to be strengthened with might by his Spirit in the inner man;
17 That Christ may dwell in your hearts by faith; that ye, being rooted and grounded in love.

(Ephesians 3:16-17 KJV)

MY FAMILY IN CHRIST (THE WORLD)

Can't Nobody Do Me Like Jesus

Is there anything on this earth that can really satisfy me?
Only you, dear Jesus, know what that can be.
I can search the world high and low,
But you are the one who can give me what I need; there is no other place for me to go.
Because there are so many earthly things that I have tried,
But I cannot think of one thing, dear Jesus, that kept me completely satisfied.
Never content and always wanting more,
Until I found you, and this kind of contentment I have never experienced before.
So, I choose to live for you this day, and every day,
Spreading your good news and making sure your word never goes away.
Because there is nothing else for me, but in you to believe and trust,
And, I know for sure that there is nothing or nobody else that can do me like you, Jesus.

* * *

Not one person on earth can bless us like Jesus! This poem was inspired by "Can't Nobody Do Me Like Jesus" by Andrae Crouch. Today, listen to this song as you read 1 Timothy 6:6-8 and reflect on how amazing God's blessings are. We came into this world with nothing, but we are so blessed. What has God given you?

6 But godliness with contentment is great gain.
7 For we brought nothing into this world, and it is certain we can carry nothing out.
8 And having food and raiment let us be therewith content.

(1 Timothy 6:6-8 KJV)

Love Theory

Lord, how do I show my love for others?
Is it a type of love for all people, my love should cover?
Is it a kind of love for people only I know?
Or is it a kind of love for all people on earth, and how deep should it go?
Is it a kind of love for people who do not like me so much?
Should I still love these same people who shriek at the thought of my touch?
Is it a kind of love that I should only show to my race?
Or should I show love to the same people who see my skin color and want to spit in my face?
And even though you gave me the heart to love all people, I must admit my heart gets weary,
Trying to show love and kindness to people who hate me, but God, I will continue to live by your love theory.

* * *

It's really hard to love people who hate us back. Those of us who have God's love in our hearts can't make sense out of this hate. With God's help, we can continue showing the world his love. Today, look up "Love Theory" by Kirk Franklin as you reflect on Matthew 5:44-45. Continue blessing those that curse you and take comfort in the love of your brothers and sisters in Christ as well as God's love. Can you put a little extra kindness in the world today?

44 But I say unto you, Love your enemies, bless them that curse you, do good to them that hate you, and pray for them which despitefully use you, and persecute you;
45 That ye may be the children of your Father which is in heaven: for he maketh his sun to rise on the evil and on the good, and sendeth rain on the just and on the unjust.
(Matthew 5:44-45 KJV)

MY FAMILY IN CHRIST (THE WORLD)

It's Working

I know that everything I am doing in my life,
Is trying to follow your word, dear Jesus, on how to be a good wife.
Trying to live my life for you,
Trying to follow all things that are true.
Even when it is hard to admit when I am wrong,
That is when I pray to be humble and not be headstrong.
Because there was a time when I did not care,
Now, dear Jesus, your words I hold so dear,
And that is why I no longer want to walk in the flesh,
I want to walk in your spirit, and I want to start my life fresh.
And I know if I were still living in my sins, I would be hurting,
But because of your Holy Spirit living inside of me now, I know that it's working.

* * *

When you set it in your heart, God is so faithful that he will help you become the good person you want to become if you make the effort. It works if you work on it. Today, look up William Murphy's song "It's Working" and listen to it as you reflect on Romans 12:2. Are you conforming to the world or rising to God's standards and being transformed?

2 And be not conformed to this world: but be ye transformed by the renewing of your mind, that ye may prove what is that good, and acceptable, and perfect, will of God.
(Romans 12:2 KJV)

Jesus I'll Never Forget

Jesus, I always felt you near me,
But I was not ready to accept you, and not realizing that to my life, you held the key.
Even when I was out there doing wrong,
You knew one day that I would come along.
To seek and find you, something that was always in my heart,
I just didn't know where to look or search; I did not know where to start.
But I knew that I was getting tired of living in my sins,
Just like you already knew where my life would end.
You were just waiting for me to let go,
Of my prideful nature and my puffed-up ego.
So that you could show me your love and favor and a life you had already set,
A life of peace and joy for me, dear Jesus, is something I will never forget.

* * *

How could we forget how much Jesus has done for us? Sometimes we do. He was born to die for our sins. He came to give us a life of abundance. Today, look up the old gospel song "Jesus, I'll Never Forget" by Sam Cooke with The Soul Stirrers as you reflect on Luke 21:28. Have you thought lately about how much Jesus has done for you?

28 And when these things begin to come to pass, then look up, and lift up your heads; for your redemption draweth nigh.

(Luke 21:28 KJV)

You Are Always Here

Lord, I feel your presence wherever I go,
Even though I can't see you, I just know.
That you are always walking with me through the good and the bad,
And you have never forsaken your protection of me, I've always had.
So that is why you are my strength and stronghold,
And my faith and trust in you I will always hold.
Because without you, I have built my house on sand alone,
And I also know that without you, it will never stand up on its own.
So that is why I will build my house on a solid foundation, and I will not fear,
Because I know, Lord, without a doubt, that you are always here.

* * *

No matter what you're doing or what you're going through, the Lord is always with you. Today, as you reflect on this poem and Hebrews 11:1-3, say a deep and heartfelt prayer for God's anointing over you and your family and friends. Look up the song "Lord, You Are Always Here with Me" by Livets Ord Worship and spend some time with the Lord. Pray he's always with you to give you the right words to say to unbelievers; the right reactions to not react in anger; and the peace and love in your heart that you need in tough situations. Do you truly believe God is always here? Believe it today, family.

1 Now faith is the substance of things hoped for, the evidence of things not seen.
2 For by it the elders obtained a good report.
3 Through faith we understand that the worlds were framed by the word of God, so that things which are seen were not made of things which do appear.

(Hebrews 11:1-3 KJV)

Nobody

I see, Lord, you seek the lowest to the high,
All types of people you use for your good and leaving us always to ask why.
Why would you choose that person who is so low?
To spread your good news and represent you, we don't know.
But only you know how to use all types of people for your own good,
Because leaving it up to us, it would be completely misunderstood.
Because we judge a person how they act and look,
But you, dear Lord, don't judge a cover but what is inside the book.
And though a person is living in sin and their world may be rocky,
You alone can make that person great when he feels like a nobody.

* * *

As you read this poem, think about how you feel when others judge you or how you judge others. Today, look up the song "Nobody" by Casting Crowns and Matthew West as you reflect on Romans 12:6-8. Only we, as humans, judge others based on looks and actions, while God looks at the heart. God needs all of us to show his love to others. Pray that others see Jesus in you.

6 Having then gifts differing according to the grace that is given to us, whether prophecy, let us prophesy according to the proportion of faith;
7 Or ministry, let us wait on our ministering: or he that teacheth, on teaching;
8 Or he that exhorteth, on exhortation: he that giveth, let him do it with simplicity; he that ruleth, with diligence; he that sheweth mercy, with cheerfulness.
(Romans 12:6-8 KJV)

MY FAMILY IN CHRIST (THE WORLD)

The Holy Ghost

When you were out in the world living in your sins,
Was there always a voice inside of you, deep within?
Trying to tell you right from wrong,
But you did not want to hear that same old song.
Even though you knew it was trying to tell you to do what was right,
You fought that voice inside of you with all your might.
Because you were not ready to change your ways,
But the voice inside of you kept telling you that living in your sin never pays.
The voice inside of you that you tried to block out,
That same voice you really do not want to be without.
So, you decided finally to follow that voice that lives inside of you like an unwanted host,
Don't worry about the voice, my friend; that is what the good Lord blessed you with—the Holy Ghost.

* * *

The Holy Spirit gives discernment as well as spiritual gifts. This is how God communicates with us. It speaks to us about what is right and wrong. It lets us know when we're somewhere we shouldn't be, or tells us to talk to someone who is in need. When you want to live in sin, you try to block out that voice, but as you welcome Jesus into your heart, you crave a deeper relationship with the Holy Ghost. Today, as you reflect on this poem and 1 Corinthians 12:8-11, listen to the song "Holy Ghost" by Joe Praize and think of how your life has evolved through your relationship with Christ. Have you grown as a Christian because of it?

8 For to one is given by the Spirit the word of wisdom; to another the word of knowledge by the same Spirit;
9 To another faith by the same Spirit; to another the gifts of healing by the same Spirit;
10 To another the working of miracles; to another prophecy; to another discerning of spirits; to another divers kinds of tongues; to another the interpretation of tongues:
11 But all these worketh that one and the selfsame Spirit, dividing to every man severally as he will.

(1 Corinthians 12:8-11 KJV)

MY FAMILY IN CHRIST (THE WORLD)

Chapter Five: Jesus Is Our Salvation

1. Your Church Is Still Alive

2. Amazing Grace

3. Trust in You Lord

4. Believers, Be Ready

5. Lord Help Me to Hold Out

6. God's Word Is True

7. Give This World Back to God

8. Still Able

9. Everything Is Gonna Be Alright

10. Stay on Jesus' Battlefield

11. What a Beautiful Name

Your Church Is Still Alive

Dear Lord, there is so much turmoil and unrest,
Coming from all over the world, east, south, north, and west.
There is no place where you won't find sin,
It just keeps repeating itself over and over again.
Even though people know that sin is wrong,
They have become slaves to their own sins because they have been doing it for so long.
So, nothing or no one matters; it is all about them,
They forgot all about God's commandments and his words; they forgot about him.
But even in this, there is always hope,
Because our Lord and Savior, Jesus Christ, left something for us to cope.
And that is his precious gift, the Holy Spirit,
We just have to let him into our lives and not fear it.
By living our lives in a righteous way and for the truth to always strive,
Because no matter what the devil does to us, dear Jesus, your church is still alive.

* * *

It's amazing that after 2000 years, the church is still alive. That's because God is real. The people of God see something real through their faith in Christ. Satan wouldn't fight so hard against us if God were not real, and he wouldn't fight so hard against Jesus if he were not God's only Son. Today, listen to Mack Brock's song "Your Church Is Alive" as you reflect on Jeremiah 17:5-8, and ask yourself if you put more faith in people or in God to get things done. Do you pray first or ask things of people first? Make it a point to start praying first, starting today.

5 Thus saith the Lord; Cursed be the man that trusteth in man, and maketh flesh his arm, and whose heart departeth from the Lord.
6 For he shall be like the heath in the desert, and shall not see when good cometh; but shall inhabit the parched places in the wilderness, in a salt land and not inhabited. 7 Blessed is the man that trusteth in the Lord, and whose hope the Lord is. 8 For he shall be as a tree planted by the waters, and that spreadeth out her roots by the river, and shall not see when heat cometh, but her leaf shall be green; and shall not be careful in the year of drought, neither shall cease from yielding fruit. (Jeremiah 17:5-8 KJV)

MY FAMILY IN CHRIST (THE WORLD)

Amazing Grace

I was living my life through the world's eyes,
Thinking I was living for you, dear Lord, but truly living for Satan in disguise.
Even though I was trying to live my life right,
I did not have your protection or suit of armor to fight.
All I had was my beliefs in what I thought was true,
But now, being filled with your Holy Spirit, I realize that I did not even know you.
Because I truly did not know your words, to keep the devil at bay,
I kept living in my sins, hoping that you would just come along and save me someday.
Without thinking that I needed to surrender all of me to you,
I thought just believing you existed was all I needed to do.
But now I realize it is much more than in you to believe,
I have to be willing to do your good works, dear Lord; I have to be willing to roll up my sleeves.
And if that means I have to travel the world from place to place,
I know that you will be leading me on, dear Jesus, through your Amazing Grace.

* * *

As Christians, we have to be willing to surrender to Christ, and willing to do the Lord's good works. "Amazing Grace" is such a great old hymn that there have been many adaptations over the years. Today, as you reflect on Ephesians 5:8-9, listen to Chris Tomlin's "Amazing Grace (My Chains Are Gone)" and consider how good the Lord has been to you. We are the light of the world. We must commit to letting Jesus lead us, and it takes work. Are you committed?

8 For ye were sometimes darkness, but now are ye light in the Lord: walk as children of light:
9 (For the fruit of the Spirit is in all goodness and righteousness and truth;).
(Ephesians 5:8-9 KJV)

Trust in You Lord

When it seems like nothing is going your way,
When things are so bad, you don't even have the heart to pray.
Living in a world full of people and you still feel so alone,
Feeling like God has left you to live life all on your own.
No one to talk to, or your feelings to share,
Living in a world all about self where no one seems to care.
So, you go through your life living alone, asking yourself what does this all mean?
Feeling like you have lived your life for so long, not being heard or seen.
But that is when you must know that God loves you and his words are true,
By lifting your hands up high and saying to the Lord, "I will only trust in you."

* * *

Over and over, the Bible tells us not to be afraid. The Lord will never fail us if we have faith in him. We go through trials of faith, and sometimes God is quiet. Today, as you reflect on Deuteronomy 31:8, look up the song "Trust in You" by Lauren Daigle and listen to it. Will you double your faith and trust in the Lord today?

8 And the Lord, he it is that doth go before thee; he will be with thee, he will not fail thee, neither forsake thee: fear not, neither be dismayed.

(Deuteronomy 31:8 KJV)

Believers, Be Ready

There are so many things in this world that we do not realize,
Just living for things in this world and not even being wise.
To the fact that God is what we should be living for,
But money, fame, wealth, and possessions are what we truly adore.
So, we keep striving for all these things in our life,
Willing to sacrifice our souls and not even think about it, twice.
And not giving it a thought that these worldly possessions will not always be around,
We keep searching for happiness in all these things, only to be let down.
And not knowing that without God, our lives will always be unsteady,
Because he wants us to be preparing and waiting on him, he wants all his believers to be ready.

* * *

God wants us all to be ready when Jesus comes riding on the cloud of glory to collect his children. Today, listen to the song "People, Get Ready" by Curtis Mayfield as you reflect on Matthew 6:19-21, and ask yourself where your treasures are laid. Are you ready for Jesus to come back? When that trumpet calls, believers had better be ready. Pray for those who are not ready today.

19 Lay not up for yourselves treasures upon earth, where moth and rust doth corrupt, and where thieves break through and steal:
20 But lay up for yourselves treasures in heaven, where neither moth nor rust doth corrupt, and where thieves do not break through nor steal:
21 For where your treasure is, there will your heart be also.

(Matthew 6:19-21 KJV)

MY FAMILY IN CHRIST (THE WORLD)

Lord Help Me to Hold Out

Living in a world where everything goes,
Trying to find God, but nobody knows.
I keep searching, but he is nowhere to be found,
Praying and calling his name, only to get silence and no sound.
So, I'm going to keep having faith that he hears what I have to say,
Dear Lord, I don't want to die in my sins; I want to be with you someday.
So, I come to you tired and heavy-hearted,
Praying and hoping that it is not too late, and your love and mercy on me have not yet departed.
And even though this world continues to live in sin and doubt,
I know someday that you will return, so with my temptations—I need you, dear Jesus, to help me to hold out.

* * *

God's word says to love the sinner, not the sin. We should never love the world more than we do God. As we grow older and more weary, it may become tiresome to hold out, but have faith in the Lord that he can give you the strength you need to hang on. Today, listen to the song "Lord, Help Me to Hold Out" by The Harold Smith Majestics as you reflect on 1 John 2:15-17. This world will pass away, but our souls are eternal. Where do you place your love? On the eternal or on the things of this world?

15 Love not the world, neither the things that are in the world. If any man love the world, the love of the Father is not in him.
16 For all that is in the world, the lust of the flesh, and the lust of the eyes, and the pride of life, is not of the Father, but is of the world.
17 And the world passeth away, and the lust thereof: but he that doeth the will of God abideth for ever.

(1 John 2:15-17 KJV)

God's Word Is True

In this world we live in today, there is so much hate,
Why can't we seem to love one another before it becomes too late?
Putting money and power above everything else,
Not caring about anyone, only looking out for self.
Why can't people realize the sacrifice that Jesus made for us to be,
Dying on that cross for our sins, he did that just for you and me.
And we should be living for him and turning away from our sinful ways,
So that we can live a life of righteousness for him for the rest of our days.
And that means turning our lives around and becoming anew,
By following God's word, which is always true.

* * *

Jesus paid the ultimate sacrifice for our sins so that we could gain eternal life with him and our Father God in heaven. It was a price we couldn't afford to pay. It isn't too much to ask that we make every effort to live our lives righteous and honest, following God's word to the best of our ability. Today, listen to Yemi Levite's song "Your Word Is True" as you reflect on 1 John 2:11, knowing that hiding darkness in your heart hinders you from becoming anew and following God's word. What sins have you been unwilling to let go?

11 But he that hateth his brother is in darkness, and walketh in darkness, and knoweth not whither he goeth, because that darkness hath blinded his eyes.

(1 John 2:11 KJV)

MY FAMILY IN CHRIST (THE WORLD)

Give This World Back to God

What is going on in this world today?
Where is the love for one another? Where has it gone? It just seems to have went away.
What has happened to us trying to feed someone that is hungry? Or helping someone in need?
Where is the Holy Spirit that our Lord and Savior, Jesus Christ, gave to each and every one of us, family; where is it indeed?
The Holy Spirit, which shows love and mercy to all human race,
That overcame hatred and sin through God's favorable grace.
We cannot allow Satan to lead our lives into such turmoil and unrest with a light so dim,
We must pray to God and turn this world back over to him.

* * *

If you can just imagine for a moment how much different this world would be if every person helped just one person in need, there wouldn't be any people left in need. Not one person would be left needing a place to sleep or a meal to eat. Today, as you reflect on this poem and Galatians 6:2, listen to Reba McEntire's song "Back to God" and think about those around you who need help. A child whose parents are struggling. An older individual on a fixed income or without a vehicle or ability to drive; perhaps you know someone with a lack of family. There are many around us in need, if we only look. The world needs more of Jesus' love. Will you help someone today?

2 Bear ye one another's burdens, and so fulfil the law of Christ.

(Galatians 6:2 KJV)

Still Able

There is so much going on in this world,
It is like a severe tornado of sin that continues to swirl.
Going round and round, out of control,
Only God has the power to forgive sin, and only he knows.
When a time will come, and sin will be no more,
When we will see Jesus coming and gladly open our doors.
Because then we will know that everything will be ok,
Because our dear Jesus will be back home to stay.
And he will never again be apart from us,
No longer will we fear death or our bodies turning into dust.
So, until Jesus comes back, I will be patient and keep my mind clear and stable,
Because I know through all of this world's troubles, Jesus can help—because he is still able.

* * *

There are several versions of the song "Still Able," so many of Christ's followers know and believe he is still able! As you reflect on this poem and Revelation 2:6 today, look up James Fortune & FIYA's version of "Still Able" and listen to it. Sin is all around us, and sometimes it's hard to avoid. It helps if we surround ourselves in fellowship with other followers of Christ. But, Jesus can still overcome all the world's troubles. We need to pray for this world. Do you pray for the world daily? Will you start, today?

6 But this thou hast, that thou hatest the deeds of the Nicolaitanes, which I also hate.
(Revelation 2:6 KJV)

MY FAMILY IN CHRIST (THE WORLD)

Everything Is Gonna Be Alright

Dear Lord, this world is not living by your word,
It appears to be falling deeper into every sin to the point that it is becoming absurd.
Where everything is acceptable and nothing is wrong,
Every sin is ok; we all just need to get along.
So, we say to each other, you do your thing and let me do mine,
We won't bother each other with our sins, and everything will be fine.
Just keep on doing whatever we feel,
Living our lives, the way we want—it is no big deal.
But for those who trust and fear the Lord with all your might,
Know that God is always working in our favor, and everything is gonna be alright.

* * *

When you have the Holy Spirit's conviction inside you, you know what is right and wrong, and you cannot stand for living in sin. We are not of this world. As Christians, we must be the light of this world and set ourselves apart, not living like everyone else and just falling into a sinful nature. Today, as you reflect on this poem and 2 Corinthians 4:4, look up Ben Tankard's version of "Everything's Gonna Be Alright" and consider your own daily walk. Is there something you're struggling with that you need to make a stand for Christ? Take a stand for Christ, today.

4 In whom the god of this world hath blinded the minds of them which believe not, lest the light of the glorious gospel of Christ, who is the image of God, should shine unto them.

(2 Corinthians 4:4 KJV)

Stay on Jesus' Battlefield

Lord, it seems like in this world today, doing wrong is right,
And standing up for truth is a fight.
Everything that appears to be good,
Is somehow bad and completely misunderstood.
And when you open up your heart to give,
Being called a fool because they don't understand how the homeless and poor people live.
Because this world believes that only the strong survives,
Not caring about God's people and believing that God's truth is all lies.
And not knowing that his word will always be true and real,
But people choose to live in their sins instead of standing firm with Jesus on his battlefield.

* * *

In the Bible, God's people were strong warriors. We, too, have to be strong and willing to stand up for what is right and just. Today, as you reflect on this poem and 1 Thessalonians 2:9-13, look up the classic gospel song "Stay on the Battlefield" as sung by the Christianaires and remind yourself that it takes more courage to take a stand for justice and do what's right than it does to go along with the rest of the world. Just because something is legal doesn't make it morally right. If more of God's people stood together today, we would make a difference in the world. Will you stand with Jesus on his battlefield?

9 For ye remember, brethren, our labour and travail: for labouring night and day, because we would not be chargeable unto any of you, we preached unto you the gospel of God.
10 Ye are witnesses, and God also, how holily and justly and unblameably we behaved ourselves among you that believe:
11 As ye know how we exhorted and comforted and charged every one of you, as a father doth his children,
12 That ye would walk worthy of God, who hath called you unto his kingdom and glory.
13 For this cause also thank we God without ceasing, because, when ye received the word of God which ye heard of us, ye received it not as the word of men, but as it is in truth, the word of God, which effectually worketh also in you that believe.

(1 Thessalonians 2:9-13 KJV)

What a Beautiful Name

Beauty comes in all shapes, colors, and forms,
But so do evil which seems to be today's norm.
Even though our Lord did not create us to be this way,
He only wanted us to praise, honor him and pray.
But we continued to be disobedient and did not care,
About following God's laws, for us they were just to much to bare.
But even then he let his will be done,
By sacrificing for us his only son.
And even though we continued to sin, he still wanted to keep in touch
And God I am so grateful that you loved us that much.
So I thank you for being so forgiving,
Because of your forgiveness, in my sins I am no longer living.
And I can say that today, tomorrow and always you remain the same,
No matter what, I will continue to praise you,
Jesus and shout to the world what a beautiful name.

* * *

Today, as you reflect on this poem and probably the most well-known verse of the entire Bible, John 3:16, look up the song "What a Beautiful Name" by Hillsong Worship. The reason Jesus' name is so beautiful is because of the great sacrifice he made for us. And, the reason John 3:16 is so prominent is because it sums up the Bible and Jesus' life so perfectly. It's the reason for all of it—why he came to earth, why he died, and how we get to heaven. Have you asked for his forgiveness? Have you told others about his great sacrifice? Tell someone today. God will give you the words to say.

16 For God so loved the world, that he gave his only begotten Son, that whosoever believeth in him should not perish, but have everlasting life.

(John 3:16 KJV)

MY FAMILY IN CHRIST (THE WORLD)

Chapter Six: Jesus – Unstoppable Peace

1. Joy of Peace in My Soul

2. Overflow

3. God You Are So Wonderful

4. Why We Sing

5. When I Rose This Morning

6. I Lift Up My Voice

7. Soon and Very Soon

8. Since I Laid My Burdens Down

9. Sunday Mornings

10. Move on Up a Little Higher

Joy of Peace in My Soul

Dear Lord, there is a peace that has taken over me,
I can feel it all over my body, even down to my feet.
It is such a peace, to the world, I can't explain,
It is a kind of peace that a person living in their sins they cannot obtain.
Because this peace comes from living in a righteous way,
Something that is so hard to come by, living in this world today.
Because people want to live in confusion and not peace,
They prefer to live in lies that Satan has unleashed.
So, they can never feel your amazing glory,
Because they want to continue living on Satan's territory.
But for me, I like the peace that you give,
The feeling of your peace, dear Lord, that is so positive.
And for the people whose peace Satan has stolen and it is now taking an emotional toll,
It is so sad for them, because they will never experience the joy of peace that you give, that I can feel in my soul.

* * *

If you have the peace of Jesus in your soul, then you know what it's like to wish everyone had that peace. It's hard seeing someone go through turmoil without the love of Jesus in their heart. Today, listen to the classic song "I've Got Peace Like a River" as sung by the Cedarmont Kids and reflect on Romans 15:13. Think of how your life was before you accepted Jesus as your Lord and Savior. Do you have that peace in your heart today?

13 May the God of hope fill you with all joy and peace in believing, that ye may abound in hope, through the power of the Holy Ghost.

(Romans 15:13 KJV)

Overflow

Dear Lord, I feel so full,
Always excited by your word, that is never dull.
Wanting to learn as much as I can,
Studying and living for you is my game plan.
Because I can never get enough of learning about you,
I don't understand how people don't believe in our Lord and Savior; I don't have a clue.
How can they not feel your Holy Spirit inside?
People doing what they want to do, and your word they will not abide.
And not caring that you will be back again,
They are only living for this world and being caught up in their sins.
But for you, my love I will continue to show,
Because your love and mercy for me are a constant overflow.

* * *

The Lord has an abundance of love and mercy for all. He never runs out. Tasha Cobbs sings a beautiful rendition of a "Fill Me Up/Overflow" medley. I encourage you to look it up today as you reflect on Psalm 1:1-6. Do you delight in the Lord? Can you imagine overflowing with his peace and love? What joy that is!

1 Blessed is the man that walketh not in the counsel of the ungodly, nor standeth in the way of sinners, nor sitteth in the seat of the scornful.
2 But his delight is in the law of the Lord; and in his law doth he meditate day and night.
3 And he shall be like a tree planted by the rivers of water, that bringeth forth his fruit in his season; his leaf also shall not wither; and whatsoever he doeth shall prosper.
4 The ungodly are not so: but are like the chaff which the wind driveth away.
5 Therefore the ungodly shall not stand in the judgment, nor sinners in the congregation of the righteous.
6 For the Lord knoweth the way of the righteous: but the way of the ungodly shall perish.
(Psalm 1:1-6 KJV)

MY FAMILY IN CHRIST (THE WORLD)

God You Are So Wonderful

I am so happy to explain what I am feeling in my heart,
How your word is truth for me and how it will never part.
And I will forever live for all that you say,
And your word, dear Lord, I will never disobey.
Because I know without you, I'm living on borrowed time,
Trying so hard to repent and leaving my old life behind.
And how being filled with your Holy Spirit has brought me so much joy,
Because it has filled my heart and soul from an empty void.
And you showed me that with you, my life will never be dull,
Always learning something new in good, because, God, you are so wonderful.

* * *

Life is so empty without Jesus. Even more, it's impossible to leave our old sinful lives behind without Jesus to fill us and guide us to a new life. His guidance teaches us a new way to live—in truth. Today, as you reflect on this poem and John 16:13, look up the old gospel song "He's So Wonderful" by Sam Cooke with The Soul Stirrers and listen to it. Do you have peace, love, and joy? Have you found God's hope? Open your heart to Jesus.

13 Howbeit when he, the Spirit of truth, is come, he will guide you into all truth: for he shall not speak of himself; but whatsoever he shall hear, that shall he speak: and he will shew you things to come.

(John 16:13 KJV)

Why We Sing

When we are close to God, there is so much joy in our hearts,
Nothing can bring us down, and the devil can't tear our faith apart.
Because when we have the Holy Spirit living inside of us,
We have God's armor of protection, and no, Satan, you cannot get through—only Jesus.
Because our Lord and Savior, Jesus Christ, is right here to defend,
As long as we continue to have faith in him, the devil cannot come in.
So, in our hearts, we must maintain our joy and gladness,
Even when we see all around us so much death and sadness.
So, Lord, our praises and songs we will continue to bring,
Worshipping and praising your goodness is why we sing.

* * *

Satan cannot get us down when we have a joyful heart full of Jesus. Today, as you reflect on this poem and Galatians 5:22-23, look up the song "Why We Sing" by Kirk Franklin and listen to it. Do you sing and worship God daily? Singing for the Lord brings joy to the soul.

22 But the fruit of the Spirit is love, joy, peace, longsuffering, gentleness, goodness, faith,
23 Meekness, temperance: against such there is no law.

(Galatians 5:22-23 KJV)

MY FAMILY IN CHRIST (THE WORLD)

When I Rose This Morning

I thank you, God, every day,
Because without you breathing life into my body, it would surely decay.
I need you for every breath I take,
Your mighty powers I will never underestimate.
And how I will not fear or be dismayed,
Because you are always with me through all things, and I should never be afraid.
Because it is written in the Bible about Jesus Christ and your story,
The one that I know, who holds all the power and deserves all the glory.
So today, I have a song to sing,
Thanking you, God, for waking me up when I rose this morning.

* * *

Praise God, we woke up to see another day! Today, look up the gospel song "When I Rose This Morning" by the Mississippi Mass Choir and listen to it as you reflect on this poem and Psalm 150:6. Do you thank God each day that you wake to see a new day? If not, start today!

6 Let every thing that hath breath praise the Lord. Praise ye the Lord.

(Psalm 150:6 KJV)

I Lift up My Voice

Thanks to you, Lord, I woke up with my heart filled with your mercy and grace,
Living in a world filled with so much hatred, in turmoil; I don't even worry about the dangers I may face.
Because I know that I am surrounded by your armor and glory,
And I will put my faith and trust in you; so for my life, I will no longer worry.
I will continue to press on and spread your good news,
And all I ask of you, dear Jesus, is that all of me you continue to use.
And don't let me get tired or faint,
Because I know your word and your good news, the devil always tries to constraint.
So, I will carry on your good works because, for me, I have no choice,
Being filled with your Holy Spirit, dear Jesus, I will continue to lift up my voice.

* * *

Today, listen to the song "I Lift up My Voice" by Frank Edwards as you reflect on John 16:33. There will be tribulation in the world, but the devil will not triumph in the end. The victory belongs to Jesus. Put your faith in the Lord. Are you filled with the Holy Spirit today? Rest assured in the Lord's peace.

33 These things I have spoken unto you, that in me ye might have peace. In the world ye shall have tribulation: but be of good cheer; I have overcome the world.
(John 16:33 KJV)

MY FAMILY IN CHRIST (THE WORLD)

Soon and Very Soon

I'm so glad that I'm at peace with my soul,
Living my life for you, dear Jesus, is my only goal.
To spread your good news to all that will listen,
To those who don't, your love and grace, they will sadly be missin'.
And how terrible it will be for those who do not hear,
Because you said that you would be returning, you made that so clear.
So, to those who want to keep living in their sins,
You don't want to be caught sleeping when Jesus comes back again.
Because it will be too late when you see him riding on the clouds,
Trying now to kneel down before him and shouting his name out loud.
But only you know, dear Jesus, when you will return, I can only assume.
By continuing to live my life as if you will be returning very soon.

* * *

"Soon and Very Soon," as the old hymn goes, we will all be going to see the King, Jesus Christ. Today, look up Andrae Crouch's version and listen to it as you reflect on this poem. The Bible clearly tells us that we must give our hearts to Christ here, on earth. We must believe, confess, and repent before we die, or before Jesus comes back, whichever comes first. None of us know when he's coming back, but we need to be ready, and if you haven't given your heart to Christ, don't delay. If you have, then pray diligently for others. None of us are guaranteed a tomorrow. As you read Romans 2:5-8 today, decide which category you fall into. Will you pray today?

5 But after thy hardness and impenitent heart treasurest up unto thyself wrath against the day of wrath and revelation of the righteous judgment of God;
6 Who will render to every man according to his deeds:
7 To them who by patient continuance in well doing seek for glory and honour and immortality, eternal life:
8 But unto them that are contentious, and do not obey the truth, but obey unrighteousness, indignation and wrath.

(Romans 2:5-8 KJV)

Since I Laid My Burdens Down

My life is so full of joy and peace,
Since I put my trust in you, dear Jesus, my sins have been released,
No more do I feel guilt or shame,
Because in my times of trouble, I call out your name.
And even when I start to worry, and my heart feels troubled,
That is when I pray to you, dear Lord, and ask that my portion of faith be doubled.
So that I can continue to trust in you and not fear,
By having faith and believing in you, Lord, knowing that you are near.
Because it is such a comfort to have you around,
Oh, what a relief it is, dear Jesus, to lay my burdens down.

* * *

It's always such a relief to lay our heavy burdens down! Today, look up the song "Glory, Glory Hallelujah" by Bishop G.E. Patterson and listen to it as you reflect on this poem and read Psalm 55:22. There is no comparison to the joy and relief of laying our burdens down. For those who are truly remorseful for their sins, the guilt weighs heavily on us. Jesus will take all that weight away. Won't you give it over to him today?

22 Cast thy burden upon the Lord, and he shall sustain thee: he shall never suffer the righteous to be moved.

(Psalm 55:22 KJV)

MY FAMILY IN CHRIST (THE WORLD)

Sunday Mornings

I remember on Sundays, getting ready for church, in my household,
Remembering a God-fearing grandmother whose love for Jesus was so bold.
Sitting in church, so young and not fully understanding what was being read,
The preacher was so boring to me, that I would fall asleep, and my beautiful grandmother popped me upside my head.
All I could think about was when church was over; and at my house, my whole family would meet,
Sitting down at my mother's table every Sunday with all kinds of good home-cooked foods to eat.
Remembering all the stories and the love that we shared,
A feeling of being secure in my home and never feeling scared.
Oh, how I miss those times going to church in all the happiness it would bring,
Praising the Lord first, and then being with family on Sunday mornings.

* * *

Our family can be a really good influence on us to help keep us on the right path if we are so lucky to have people like that. Even if you didn't have that growing up, you can be that person for the young people in your life. You can be that good influence on the next, younger generation. It makes more of a difference than you realize. Today, look up the song "Sunday Morning Medley" by the Georgia Mass Choir as you reflect on 1 Corinthians 10:31. Remember to do everything that you do for the glory of God. Do you know someone you can take under your wing?

31 Whether therefore ye eat, or drink, or whatsoever ye do, do all to the glory of God.
(1 Corinthians 10:31 KJV)

MY FAMILY IN CHRIST (THE WORLD)

Move on up a Little Higher

Dear Lord, my thoughts are being with you someday,
A picture of calm waters around me, sitting on the dock of a bay.
With the wind blowing slightly in my hair and the sun shining on my face,
Living a life of peace and not trying to keep up with the world's fast pace.
But taking my time because with you there are no worries,
No longer thinking about trying to get from place to place in a hurry.
Because I know being with you everything will be calm,
Just reading the praises of you in the book of psalm,
About how much you are loved, honored, and glorified,
Thinking how wonderful it is going to be someday to actually stand by your side.
So, getting closer to you is what I will continue to desire,
Living my life to do what is right, so to you, I can move on a little higher.

* * *

Someday we'll no longer have to keep up with the hustle and bustle of the world. The old gospel song "Move on up a Little Higher" has inspired many through the years, and today would be a great day to look up the version by Mahalia Jackson as you reflect on Colossians 3:1-4. Can you imagine being with Christ in glory?

1 If ye then be risen with Christ, seek those things which are above, where Christ sitteth on the right hand of God.
2 Set your affection on things above, not on things on the earth.
3 For ye are dead, and your life is hid with Christ in God.
4 When Christ, who is our life, shall appear, then shall ye also appear with him in glory.
(Colossians 3:1-4 KJV)

MY FAMILY IN CHRIST (THE WORLD)

MY FAMILY IN CHRIST (THE WORLD)

Chapter Seven: God's Favor

1. I Have You in My Life Now

2. God Is My Way Maker

3. How Can This Be?

4. Lord You Hold Out Your Hand

5. Anything Can Happen

6. My Spiritual Gift

7. You Say

8. Your Love

9. Amazing

10. Because You Loved Me

11. Known

MY FAMILY IN CHRIST (THE WORLD)

I Have You in My Life Now

Lord, there are so many things that I am going through,
I feel that I am being judged by others because I want to live my life for you.
They try to bring up my worldly past,
By telling me that following you and your word, that it will not last.
And all these things that I am doing are just for show,
People keep trying to hold me to my past, and they won't let it go.
Because they refuse to believe that I am changed,
They can't accept that, for you, my sins I have exchanged.
And the person of my past I had to leave,
That person no longer exists; why can't they just believe?
And see me for the person you have allowed me to become,
Why can't people see that your love and mercy are for everyone?
So, I keep thinking that I have to convince people that I have changed, and I keep asking myself how?
Then I realize, why bother; because you know what is in the heart, dear Jesus, and I have you in my life now.

* * *

God is always faithful, more faithful than we can ever imagine. It gives us a goal to aspire to be for others but, makes us think we have to convince others of our change. Just remember, it's the Holy Spirit's job to convict and convince. God will do the work; you just be the best example you can be. You may fall short, and you may stumble; just pray for God's strength to maintain your Christian walk. Today, listen to your favorite praise and worship songs. Find some new ones to add to your favorites list. As you reflect on this poem and 1 John 1:9, consider your daily walk. Where can you improve your walk today?

9 If we confess our sins, he is faithful and just to forgive us our sins, and to cleanse us from all unrighteousness.

(1 John 1:9 KJV)

God Is My Way Maker

How many of you know that God is truly good?
Looking back on your past troubles, you realize that he really understood.
About all the things you went through in your past,
Remembering a small voice whispering to you that your troubles would not last.
And even though you could not see your way out of your situation,
God was always there with you through all of your life's frustrations.
By letting you see that Satan was always a liar and a taker,
And keeping you standing strong in your faith, knowing that God is truly the way maker.

* * *

God is truly amazing at how he works in our lives! Today, as you reflect on this poem and Isaiah 43:16, look up the song "Way Maker" by Sinach. What a beautiful and peaceful thought knowing that God is truly the way maker in our lives. No matter what situation is weighing on your heart, God will find a way. Are you standing strong in your faith today?

16 Thus saith the Lord, which maketh a way in the sea, and a path in the mighty waters.
(Isaiah 43:16 KJV)

How Can This Be?

Lord, I ask myself over and over again,
Why do you show me so much mercy and treat me as your friend?
Because every time I come to you, you never turn me away,
Always whispering a kind word to me, even when I don't deserve what you say.
But like a good friend, you never stay mad,
Always standing right there with me, through the good and the bad.
And even when I don't deserve the kindness you show,
You are always there with me wherever I go.
And like a good friend, you stick to me like glue,
A friendship so sweet as honeydew.
But when I am wrong, you have no problems correcting me,
But you still show me so much love, dear Lord, how can this be?

* * *

God shows us what true love really is. As humans, we are flawed and led by our emotions. God corrects us out of his great love for us and only wants the best for our futures. Even then, he still shows us so much love and sets the example of how we should treat others. Today, look up "How Can It Be" by Lauren Daigle and listen to it as you reflect on this poem and Proverbs 17:17. Then, think about what kind of friend you are. How can you be a better friend?

17 A friend loveth at all times, and a brother is born for adversity.

(Proverbs 17:17 KJV)

MY FAMILY IN CHRIST (THE WORLD)

Lord You Hold Out Your Hand

Thank you, Lord, for lifting me up,
You poured all your love and mercy for me in your loving cup.
You never let me down, and you were always with me through every step,
Catching me with a safety net, you always kept.
Always watching over me when I would cry,
Wiping away my tears and helping me to stand strong and to get by.
Never leaving me in my time of need,
Always pouring out your love for me and showing me your good deeds.
Showing me that I was your child always,
Helping me out of difficult situations and leaving me amazed.
So, I thank you, Lord, for all that you have done,
I feel so special to you, but I know that I am not the only one.
Because you show love and mercy to all you can,
To the people that believe and trust in you, dear Lord, you hold out your hand.

* * *

God has never-ending love and mercy. As you read this poem today, reflect on 1 Thessalonians 5:16-18 and think about these daily tasks. To rejoice daily, pray without ceasing, and give thanks in all situations. Look up the song "I Need You to Hold My Hand" by The Jackson Southernaires and think about your daily walk with Christ. Do you trust the Lord? He's holding out his hand for you.

16 Rejoice evermore.
17 Pray without ceasing.
18 In every thing give thanks: for this is the will of God in Christ Jesus concerning you.
(1 Thessalonians 5:16-18 KJV)

Anything Can Happen

When you feel like you have your whole life planned out,
God can step into your life and do a one-eighty-degree turnabout.
When you thought your life was going in one direction only,
You now realize that God had been changing your life slowly.
Even though you did not see the direction for your life God was taking,
His plans for your life were already in the making.
So, all you can do is trust God and go along for the ride,
Stop trying to hold onto something that was not meant for you and let go of your pride.
Because God wants you to reach your fullest potential and height,
But you keep trying to hold on to your dream, and you are missing out on the true thing that is there in your sight.
And yes, even though your lost dream was your passion,
You must know that God will never forsake you, and with him by your side, anything can happen.

* * *

God always knows what's best for you, and sometimes it's best to let go and let God take control. Today, look up Jonathan Nelson's song "Anything Can Happen" and listen to it while you think about your relationship with God. As you reflect on this poem and Proverbs 19:21, ask yourself what you need to let go of. Will you let God take control today? You'll be glad you did.

21 There are many devices in a man's heart; nevertheless the counsel of the Lord, that shall stand.

(Proverbs 19:21 KJV)

My Spiritual Gift

I always knew that there was something special about me,
Something so deep inside that just wanted to be free.
And no matter how much I ran and tried,
I could not escape that voice deep inside.
Telling me that my life had just begun,
I did not understand because all the years I have worked, dear Lord, I just knew that my work was done.
And all I wanted to do was sit back and do nothing,
But you already made plans for me, and for you; I was going to do something.
So, you told me that there was something in me that you still needed to uplift,
The one thing that I had been running and hiding from my whole life—my blessed spiritual gift.

* * *

Imagine if a baby never grew, learned, or matured. He or she would never learn how to talk, communicate, dress themselves, or feed themselves. They would stay dependent on their parents, or someone, for the rest of their lives. When we become Christians, we start out as babies in faith, learning and growing, and eventually, we learn our own spiritual gifts. If we remained as babies and never learned or grew in our faith, we would neglect our gift. Today, listen to Donald Lawrence's song "The Gift" while you worship the Lord. As you reflect on this poem and 1 Timothy 4:14, think of your spiritual gift. Have you discovered it yet?

14 Neglect not the gift that is in thee, which was given thee by prophecy, with the laying on of the hands of the presbytery.

(1 Timothy 4:14 KJV)

You Say

When I feel like something, for me, seems impossible,
You remind me, dear Lord, that with you, I am unstoppable.
And that you will always be here, and not to be afraid,
Because your plan for me, with your life, dear Jesus, has already been paid.
And even though I do not know where your plans will lead,
You took that sacrifice on a cross, and my sins were freed.
So that I don't have to be a slave to my sins anymore, that is what you meant,
And not giving in to temptation, and now I am confident.
That I will live my life your way,
By living with your Holy Spirit and listening to every word that you say.

* * *

The Lord does not withhold anything good from us. For those of us with a truly humbled heart, it's easy to get into the mindset that we don't deserve good things. Today, as you reflect on this poem and Job 42:2, look up the song "You Say" by Lauren Daigle and listen to it. Do you believe the word of the Lord today? You deserve to be blessed. You are loved by the Lord.

2 I know that thou canst do every thing, and that no thought can be withholden from thee.
(Job 42:2 KJV)

Your Love

God, I try to understand why you chose me,
I did not do anything special that I could see.
That you would shine all your glory my way,
It seems like all my life, from you, I was running away.
But, for whatever reason, you would not let me go,
Instead, you filled me with your Holy Spirit, and it just continued to grow.
So now, my heart and soul are full of joy,
Spreading your good news to others is now what I enjoy.
And I will always lift my hands to you above,
Because I see now that my life would be in ruins without your love.

* * *

We think when we give our lives to Christ, we are choosing our path, but this is not the case. According to John 15:16, WE are chosen by Jesus. He chose YOU. So, though we think we are in charge of our lives, and we do have free will, God made us, and Jesus chooses us and the path we are supposed to take. As you reflect on this poem today, look up the song "Your Love" by William Murphy and listen to it. Remember, the result of choosing to answer God's call is to choose the path to ultimate peace and love through all circumstances. Won't you choose Jesus today?

16 (Jesus said) Ye have not chosen me, but I have chosen you, and ordained you, that ye should go and bring forth fruit, and that your fruit should remain: that whatsoever ye shall ask of the Father in my name, he may give it you.

(John 15:16 KJV)

Amazing

Lord, you have been so good to me,
You continue to show me all that I can be
Even when I can't see, and I have my doubts,
You keep pushing me closer to you and showing me what I am all about.
Telling me not to be afraid and to keep going,
Your wonderful love and mercy for me, you just keep on showing.
And even when I want to give up,
You tell me to keep living for you, and you will always be my backup.
So, dear Lord, your name I will continue worshipping and praising,
Because all the things you have and continue to do in my life, Jesus, are simply amazing.

* * *

God is so good! Today, as you reflect on this poem and read Psalm 86:5, consider how good God has been in your life. Look up the song "Amazing" by Ricky Dillard & New G and think about how amazing God truly is in your life. What has he done for you? Don't you just want to tell everybody? Be sure to thank him today!

5 For thou, Lord, art good, and ready to forgive; and plenteous in mercy unto all them that call upon thee.

(Psalm 86:5 KJV)

Because You Loved Me

You showed me all the things that I could reach,
By spreading your good news to others, I never thought I would teach.
Because I never thought that I could have a voice,
I did not think I knew enough about you to offer others a choice.
But you told me that I could do anything and all I had to do was try,
To go out on faith and trust in you, and for me your message you would supply.
So, that is what I did; I went out on faith,
By spreading your good news, and your Holy Spirit I did embrace.
And I still have to ask myself, how could all of this be?
And then I hear a quiet voice whisper that says, "because you loved me."

* * *

He did it all because he loves you! Today, look up the song "Because You Loved Me" by Celine Dion as you reflect on this poem and Mark 16:15. Ask yourself what you can do for Jesus, because you love him, too. Do you tell others about Christ? Think of who needs to hear about Christ and be a witness for him, starting today.

15 And he said unto them, Go ye into all the world, and preach the gospel to every creature.
(Mark 16:15 KJV)

Known

Lord, it seemed like you knew me before I was born,
An unfailing love that you have for me that was never torn.
Even though I have not always played by your rules,
Walking away from you like so many other fools.
Not taking time out to give you all the glory and praise,
You still were loving and holding on to me, in spite of my sinful ways.
And you knew what kind of person that I was going to become,
I just didn't see it because I was so blind and spiritually dumb.
Living in my sins all my life and not caring what happened next,
Living a life of confusion and making my world so complex.
But for me, your loving mercy you have always shown,
And I know now that by you, I was always known.

* * *

How amazing that God has always known each and every one of us. Today, as you reflect on Psalm 37:23-24, look up the song "Known" by Tauren Wells. The Lord has always known who we were destined to become, when we would stumble, and will always be there to help us. Are you walking with the Lord today?

23 The steps of a good man are ordered by the Lord: and he delighteth in his way.
24 Though he fall, he shall not be utterly cast down: for the Lord upholdeth him with his hand.

(Psalm 37:23-24 KJV)

MY FAMILY IN CHRIST (THE WORLD)

Chapter Eight: Working for the Lord

1. I Will Praise You in This Storm

2. You Won't Let Me Go

3. Showed Me Your Love

4. Fill Me Up

5. Your Holy Spirit

6. No Weapon

7. My God Is Awesome

8. I Woke Up With My Mind Staying on Jesus

9. I'm Not Tired Yet

10. Something About Your Wonderful Name

I Will Praise You in This Storm

Dear Lord, when I think my life could not get any worse,
When there is trouble all around me, I take my comfort in a Bible verse.
Because in your words are protection and truth,
And I know this by your Holy Spirit, living inside of me as proof.
Because even though I am surrounded by evil,
Where sins of this world have caused it to be in an upheaval.
Because lies have been turned into truth, and truth has been turned into violence,
So many people are afraid to stand up for righteousness, so now their voices have gone silent.
And all that is left is confusion and distrust,
The devil has made it all about him and has caused division between us.
So, now fear and hatred have become our norm,
But I know, dear Jesus, that you are in control, so I will praise you in this storm.

* * *

Today, as you read this poem, think of the song "Praise You in This Storm" recorded by Casting Crowns. Consider listening to it as you reflect on Romans 1:18. How difficult it is to raise our hands in worship when we've been beaten down in the storms of life. It's also difficult to stand up for what's right, especially when you stand alone. Often, if you stand up, others will stand with you. Even if you are alone, it's still so rewarding, for Jesus is still in control, and in the end, his righteousness stands firm, forever. Stand fast, in his love. Won't you overcome your fears?

18 For the wrath of God is revealed from heaven against all ungodliness and unrighteousness of men, who hold the truth in unrighteousness.

(Romans 1:18 KJV)

MY FAMILY IN CHRIST (THE WORLD)

You Won't Let Me Go

Dear Lord, when I feel like from this world, I want to retreat,
You show me how much there is to live for, and you give my soul peace.
Even when things are not getting any better,
You remind me that you are with me forever.
So, I hold on to that thought with all my might,
And when I feel the walls closings in on me, I hold onto your words, oh, so tight.
Because I know without you this world I could not take,
There is not enough love in this world but a lot of lonely heartache.
Because people don't take the time out for one another,
They seemed to have forgotten that you wanted us to love as sisters and brothers.
And to give all people a helping hand,
It seems like we forgot all about this when you moved us into your promised land.
But one thing I will not forget and this I know,
You promised that if I trust, believe, and come back to you, that you won't let me go.

* * *

All God wants from us is our love and trust in him. Today, as you reflect on this poem and Psalm 91:14-16, look up the song "You Won't Let Me Go" by Stephen Miller and listen to it. Think about how God never lets you go through all the good times and the bad. We forget about God so often, but he never forgets about us. Won't you hold tighter to God today?

14 Because he hath set his love upon me, therefore will I deliver him: I will set him on high, because he hath known my name.
15 He shall call upon me, and I will answer him: I will be with him in trouble; I will deliver him, and honour him.
16 With long life will I satisfy him, and shew him my salvation.

(Psalm 91:14-16 KJV)

Showed Me Your Love

My life has been changed since I discovered you,
Dear Lord, I have never experienced something so wonderful and new.
It is as though I am seeing some things for the very first time,
Wanting to live a new life and leaving my sins behind.
By not getting upset over every little thing,
But having a sense of calmness that only your Holy Spirit can bring.
I never thought this kind of peace could exist,
Because I always worried about the things in my life that I did not trust you to fix.
But now, I am finally seeing so many things so clear,
And now, I refuse to live my life being worried or in fear.
So, Lord, how great you are is what I will speak of,
How you opened my eyes to see and showed me your love.

* * *

God is so amazing how he shows us his great love and gives us peace in our hearts. Today, look up John Legend's song "Show Me" as you reflect on this poem and John 14:27. Think about how much you really trust God to take care of things in your life. He doesn't want us to worry over anything. You still have to do the work, but you shouldn't worry about the outcome. Do you trust him to take care of you today?

27 Peace I leave with you, my peace I give unto you: not as the world giveth, give I unto you. Let not your heart be troubled, neither let it be afraid.

(John 14:27 KJV)

Fill Me Up

Help me, dear Lord, to continue to do your good works,
Always giving you the praise, glory, and honor, and not being deceived by worldly perks.
By not leaning on my own understanding, but on you, I will lean,
Trying not to get worldly possessions through my own selfish means.
But to live by your words and your words alone,
By not living my life in the sins I have always known.
Because at the time I did not understand,
That my lost soul was in your forgiving hands.
And I was not thinking about living with you always,
Not realizing that the devil was attacking me in so many ways.
So, now I seek you, and I pray that I can drink from your loving cup,
Because with your Holy Spirit, dear Jesus, it's what I need to fill me up.

* * *

Will Reagan's song "Fill Me Up" has been performed by many artists, but it is an inspiring song. Listen to it today and reflect on this poem and Colossians 3:23 as you think about how Jesus holds your soul in his forgiving hands. Do you do all things with all your might for the Lord?

23 And whatsoever ye do, do it heartily, as to the Lord, and not unto men.

(Colossians 3:23 KJV)

MY FAMILY IN CHRIST (THE WORLD)

Your Holy Spirit

My Lord, I try to do what is right in your eyes,
Always walking in your truth and not using deception as a disguise.
And even when your truth, no one wants to hear,
I will still shout your truth loud and clear.
Because I know that the devil is out to deceive,
Spreading a world full of lies is all he wants us to believe.
For anyone who will listen, his soul he wants to catch,
By removing any faith you have in God, he wants to detach.
So, for me, the devil I will continue to battle,
And I know that without you, dear Lord, my soul is very fragile.
Because the devil's lies are so easy to seem fact,
He is telling people to live in their sins, and they don't realize that their souls are constantly under attack.
But for me and my temptations, I will continue to fight it,
By praying constantly, and living with your Holy Spirit.

* * *

    Satan is truly the father of lies and will use any means to deceive all people that their sins are okay. It's so sad to see how evil people justify their actions! They often blame other people for their wrongdoing. The only way to change our behavior is by accepting and confessing our sins and repenting of those sins. Satan tries to convince us it wasn't our fault. Today, look up the song "Holy Spirit" by Kari Jobe (featuring Cody Carnes) and listen to it as you reflect on this poem and John 8:44. Remember that the Holy Spirit is a spirit of discernment, and it never lies. If you feel guilt for your choices and you're at war within yourself, it's because Satan is trying to lie to you. Cling to the Holy Spirit and do what is right. Won't you make the right decision today?

44 Ye are of your father the devil, and the lusts of your father ye will do. He was a murderer from the beginning, and abode not in the truth, because there is no truth in him. When he speaketh a lie, he speaketh of his own: for he is a liar, and the father of it.

(John 8:44 KJV)

No Weapon

My God, you are my strength and my stronghold,
Your word I will live by always, and for me, it will never grow old.
And no matter what this world has become,
Your will, for me, was always done.
Because you held out your arms like a protected shield,
And your love and mercy, for me, you've always revealed.
By letting me know that even though evil was all around me,
You were always ready to protect your child from the evil you could foresee.
So, I thank you, Lord, for keeping your loving arms wrapped around me so tight,
Every day when I am awake, and even when I go to sleep at night.
And you, dear Jesus, always looking down on me from heaven,
By not letting any evil form against me, or any weapon.

* * *

No matter what troubles or enemies we face, Jesus protects us with his grace. Today, look up the old gospel song "No Weapon" by Fred Hammond as you reflect on this poem and Psalm 138:7. No matter what weapons our enemies think they have against us, we can rest easy in Jesus' loving arms. You just need to trust him. Will you trust him today?

7 Though I walk in the midst of trouble, thou wilt revive me: thou shalt stretch forth thine hand against the wrath of mine enemies, and thy right hand shall save me.
(Psalm 138:7 KJV)

My God Is Awesome

Right now, Lord, I feel so angry and hurt,
Trying so hard not to sin because of the evil words in my mind, I just want to blurt.
Wanting to say all the things that I'm feeling in my heart and mind right now,
But because of the love I have for you, to my knees, I will take a bow.
And keep praying and asking you to forgive me of my sins,
Because no matter what, I will continue to bow to you over and over again.
And even though there is still work in me to be done,
I know with you by my side, dear Lord, that your good works in me have already begun.
And because of you Jesus, I am a flower that continues to blossom,
You keep helping me to grow in your Holy Spirit, and for me, my God, you are truly awesome.

* * *

It's so easy to sin when we're angry because anger causes an impulsive and immediate emotional response. As you reflect on this poem, look up the song "Awesome" by Charles Jenkins & Fellowship Chicago and listen to it. There are so many verses in the Bible regarding anger, but today, reflect on
Psalm 37:8 and pray for God to help you cease from anger and forsake all wrath. Don't let Satan win. Can you give God your anger today?

8 Cease from anger, and forsake wrath: fret not thyself in any wise to do evil.
(Psalm 37:8 KJV)

MY FAMILY IN CHRIST (THE WORLD)

I Woke Up With My Mind Staying on Jesus

Jesus, the first thing I do when I wake up is pray,
Praying that you will walk with me today.
Even if things don't go as I planned,
That you will not give the devil the upper hand.
By letting me lose faith in all that you have done,
Knowing that the devil has no power over me, because your victory over death has already been won.
So, I will continue to give thanks to you for everything,
For all of your love, blessings, and joy that you always bring.
And I know with you if I seek, I shall find,
By waking up every morning searching for your word, and with you, dear Jesus, staying on my mind.

* * *

Do you wake up with Jesus on your mind? Today, look up the old hymn "Woke Up This Morning With My Mind On Jesus" and reflect on 2 Corinthians 2:11. When you give your life to Christ, and you really experience a genuine change, you can't help but wake up thinking about Jesus. And it certainly helps to start your day off on the right foot to keep the devil at bay. Do you give thanks to Jesus every day? Today is a great day to start.

11 Lest Satan should get an advantage of us: for we are not ignorant of his devices.
(2 Corinthians 2:11 KJV)

I'm Not Tired Yet

Yes, Lord, I will continue to serve you,
Working to always spread your good news.
And even when I get tired and discouraged,
With you, I will continue with strength and courage.
I will not let anything or anyone lead me astray,
Because your words I will continue to obey.
From now until the end of time,
I finally realized that my life is yours and not mine.
So, I will continue doing your good works and not complain,
Telling the world how you forgave a sinner like me and freed me from my chains.
Because I know that my life has already been set,
And I just want you to know, dear Jesus, working for you—I am not tired yet.

* * *

Today, as you reflect on this poem, look up the gospel song "I'm Not Tired Yet" by Mississippi Mass Choir and give it a listen, as it's sure to put you in a good mood for the day. As you read Deuteronomy 11:13, consider how you can love and serve the Lord with all your heart and soul, and rest assured that he will renew your strength daily. Get excited for the Lord. Do you allow others to lead you astray?

13 And it shall come to pass, if ye shall hearken diligently unto my commandments which I command you this day, to love the Lord your God, and to serve him with all your heart and with all your soul.

(Deuteronomy 11:13 KJV)

Something About Your Wonderful Name

Ever since I have studied your word,
There is nothing else so true than what I have heard.
About your good news that you have prepared,
For every believer to be aware.
That we should live our lives by your word until you come,
Wishing that we all would follow your word instead of some.
But I know that there are some people that will be left behind,
Because your word of truth, they will no longer try to seek or find.
Instead, living a life of lies and not caring about the damage it leaves in its way,
Letting the devil lead them into sin, and now, with their souls, they will have to pay.
But for me, dear Jesus, I will follow and trust in you, and I will continue to proclaim,
Shouting to the world that there is something wonderful about your name.

* * *

There is something truly wonderful about Jesus' name. As you think about this poem today, look up the song "Something about the Name Jesus" by The Rance Allen Group (featuring Kirk Franklin) and reflect on Revelation 1:3. Imagine how different the world could be if everyone followed God's word. But, the world is getting further and further away from him. Will you pray for others daily? The world needs our prayers.

3 Blessed is he that readeth, and they that hear the words of this prophecy, and keep those things which are written therein: for the time is at hand.

(Revelation 1:3 KJV)

MY FAMILY IN CHRIST (THE WORLD)

Chapter Nine: The Healing Savior

1. I Need You Now

2. Dear Lord, Have Mercy

3. Till We Meet Again

4. Jesus Promised Me a Place Over There

5. Take Me to the King

6. Jesus Promised Me a Home

7. I Can Imagine

I Need You Now

Dear Lord, my body is so weak,
The doctors are saying that the sickness in my body has come to its final peak.
That there is nowhere else that I can go,
The doctors have given up, telling me that my illness—they just don't know.
And there is nothing else that they can do for me, and it is out of their hands,
They can't explain to me why my whole body is swollen; even my glands.
And all they can do is give me something for pain,
But they can't tell me why this illness is now attacking my brain.
So, I look at this, and I see no hope,
But then I realize that is when the devil starts talking, and I have to tell that devil—nope.
That I am not willing to just give up and die,
I refuse to listen to the devil's gloom and doom lie.
Because I know that my God will heal me somehow,
And, dear Lord, you need to know that I need you now.

* * *

The song "I Need You Now," originally performed by Smokie Norful, has been sung by several artists over the years, but today would be a good day to look it up and give it a listen. Most of us have gone through some illness, or maybe you're currently going through something right now. Perhaps you know someone who has cancer or another debilitating illness. As you reflect on Psalm 107:19-20, just know that God will deliver you or your loved one. Have you asked him for his healing today? Don't lose hope.

19 Then they cry unto the Lord in their trouble, and he saveth them out of their distresses.
20 He sent his word, and healed them, and delivered them from their destructions.
(Psalm 107:19-20 KJV)

MY FAMILY IN CHRIST (THE WORLD)

Dear Lord, Have Mercy

Dear Lord, sometimes this pain I cannot bear,
The devil is constantly in my head, blaming you and telling me that it is not fair.
That I should have to go through this suffering and pain,
The devil is in my head asking me why am I placing my hope in you, dear Lord, what is there for me to gain?
He keeps asking me how I can put my trust in you?
He keeps reminding me of how I am suffering and asking me what is your God going to do?
But I know the devil just wants you to blame,
And even through my sickness, I will continue to praise your name.
Because I know in my weakness, in you I am strong,
And the devil will never be able to tell me anything that you do, dear Lord, is wrong.
So, I know that you are who I have to put my faith in,
Because I know the devil's time here on earth is temporary, but you, dear Jesus, your kingdom will never end.
So, I pray that my faith in you is enough to show that I am worthy,
And in my time of sickness, dear Lord, that you will have mercy.

* * *

When you put your faith in the Almighty, you gain his strength, for he has all power. Satan knows this, and that is why he tries to make you doubt the Lord. Satan's reign on earth is temporary, but so are our infirmities. As you reflect on this poem and 2 Corinthians 12:10 today, look up the song "Have Mercy, Dear Lord" by The Williams Brothers and listen to it. Consider what is going on in your life currently. What do you need to call on the power of the Lord for today?

10 Therefore I take pleasure in infirmities, in reproaches, in necessities, in persecutions, in distresses for Christ's sake: for when I am weak, then am I strong.
(2 Corinthians 12:10 KJV)

MY FAMILY IN CHRIST (THE WORLD)

Till We Meet Again

Lord, how do I deal with my grief and loss,
How do I turn my pain over to you, dear Jesus, the one who loved me and sacrificed his life on a cross?
When I can't seem to get past my pain and grief,
Everyone keeps telling me to trust in you, and someday in my pain, I will find relief.
But I can't seem to see past what was taken away,
I want my loved one who died to come back home with me to stay.
And nothing right now can comfort my heart,
I don't know how to move on, dear Lord; I don't even know where to start.
But eventually, I know that I will have to come to you,
Because I know that there is no other way that I can see this through.
Even though all of this heartache and pain I still feel,
I know that I have to put my trust in you, dear Lord, in order for my heart to heal.
And knowing someday I will see my loved one, even though I don't know when,
It is a comfort to my heart knowing, dear Jesus, that you are watching over me and my loved one—till we meet again.

***

Losing a loved one is so hard, especially when all we want is to talk to them again. Matthew 5:4 promises us that we will be comforted when we are mourning a loss. Time does heal the pain of loss, but it never takes it away completely. The only thing you can do is face the pain and let yourself grieve. That grief lets you know that person's life had meaning. And if that person gave their life to Christ, you know you will see them again. Today, look up the song "Till We Meet Again" by Kirk Franklin and listen to it. We must share the good news of Christ with others.

4 Blessed are they that mourn: for they shall be comforted.

(Matthew 5:4 KJV)

MY FAMILY IN CHRIST (THE WORLD)

Jesus Promised Me a Place Over There

Dear Lord, my eyes can't seem to cry,
Even though I know the one I love is gone, you told us that it was not goodbye.
Because you said where you are, there is a place for all,
As long as we have faith and believe in you, not one of us would fall.
So, knowing this, how can I be sad?
Because having faith and believing in you, dear Lord, is something my loved one always had.
And even though they are gone, and there is this empty space,
My heart is filled with peace that my loved one is saved through your amazing grace.
And they will never have to worry about this world again,
About falling into temptation because of this world's sins.
And knowing that my loved one knew of your love and mercy and they were completely aware,
How they lived a righteous life because you promised them a place with you, dear Jesus, over there.

* * *

Sometimes when we lose a loved one, we can be blinded by the pain of loss. It's comforting when we know we will see our loved ones again someday. Today, look up Jennifer Hudson's version of the gospel song "Jesus Promised Me a Home over There" as you reflect on this poem and 1 Thessalonians 4:13-14 and take comfort in knowing that our Lord always keeps his promises.

13 But I would not have you to be ignorant, brethren, concerning them which are asleep, that ye sorrow not, even as others which have no hope.
14 For if we believe that Jesus died and rose again, even so them also which sleep in Jesus will God bring with him.

(1 Thessalonians 4:13-14 KJV)

MY FAMILY IN CHRIST (THE WORLD)

Take Me to the King

Someday, Lord, I will see you sitting high on your throne,
Because my heart would be filled with your love and not a heart of stone.
And I know that I cannot keep living a life of sin,
Because when that day comes, I want you to be able to let me in.
Into your kingdom, dear Jesus, where life is forever,
Where pain and suffering I will not have to endure; never.
And where I can live a life of peace,
Where all of your glory, dear Jesus, will finally be released.
And I will praise and worship you every day, for I will sing,
With a voice full of joy and happiness, shouting gladly, take me to the King.

* * *

Do you spend your days thinking about seeing Jesus? Today, as you reflect on Matthew 6:33, look up the song "Take Me to the King" by Tamela Mann and give it a listen. Each day we should be seeking first the kingdom of God and all his righteousness, and our hearts will truly become content because our desires will align with God's desires. Then, he will truly bless our lives. He always wants the best for us. Do you praise and worship God daily?

33 But seek ye first the kingdom of God, and his righteousness; and all these things shall be added unto you.

(Matthew 6:33 KJV)

MY FAMILY IN CHRIST (THE WORLD)

Jesus Promised Me a Home

Jesus, you told me to follow you,
Because there is a place that is wonderful and new.
A place where there is no more pain and sorrow,
A place I will live forever, and I don't have to worry about tomorrow.
A place where there is peace and love,
A place where no one will ever feel unloved.
A place where people will come together as one,
A place where hatred and violence are never done.
A place where there are no worries and you are never alone,
Yes, dear Jesus, you promised us someday to live in your home.

* * *

If you've never been in a mansion, much less lived in a mansion, that's okay. Dream big. Jesus has prepared a mansion in heaven so big and beautiful that our minds cannot fathom it here on earth. Today, look up the old hymn "Jesus Promised Me a Home" as you reflect on John 14:2. Imagine all the peace, love, and family you have ever known on this earth. No more pain, no more sorrow. Can you imagine all God's people coming together as one?

2 In my Father's house are many mansions: if it were not so, I would have told you. I go to prepare a place for you.

(John 14:2 KJV)

I Can Imagine

I see myself standing there looking up at the skies,
I am so deep in my thoughts about you, dear Jesus, I close my eyes.
Wondering what you are doing up there in heaven above,
I want to tell you so much in person, dear Jesus; by me, you are truly loved.
And I cannot wait to someday see your face,
Because I know how much I am loved by you, through your Amazing Grace.
And even though I cannot see your face right now,
I will continue to live by your words, and the world's sins in my life—I will not allow.
Because to see you one day is my dream,
And I know I have to keep my faith in you to be on your eternal team.
And I am going to do all I can, to do what is right and make it happen,
To stand there in your wonderful glory someday, Jesus, I can only imagine.

* * *

Have you ever imagined what it will be like when you pass on to your eternal home? Greeting your loved ones that have gone on before you, then, finally seeing Jesus on his throne? The famous song "I Can Only Imagine" by MercyMe has reached millions, and was even the title of the movie, based on true events. Today, consider watching the movie, then reflect on how amazing and awesome that will be to meet our loved ones and Jesus in heaven on that day. We don't want anyone to miss out on making heaven their eternal home. Who can you share Jesus with today?

4 And they shall see his face; and his name shall be in their foreheads.

(Revelation 22:4 KJV)

MY FAMILY IN CHRIST (THE WORLD)

Chapter Ten: The Alpha & Omega
(Beginning & Ending)

1. Son of Heaven
2. God's Got the World in His Hands
3. God's Truth and Goodness
4. Everlasting God
5. Jesus Saves
6. In the Name of Jesus
7. See You Again
8. Not Believing That Jesus Is Real
9. He's Always Right on Time
10. Lord Your Word of Truth Has Always Been Good
11. God

Son of Heaven

Dear Jesus you came into this world to save,
But the love and respect, to you the people never gave.
Instead they beat you and spit in your face,
Not wanting to believe in you so they continued to chase,
Trying to chase you down and kill you at every turn,
Not willing to hear any of your concerns.
Because they did not want to hear the truth only lies,
They did not see that your father in heaven sent you because of their cries.
Instead they wanted to believe that everything you said was false,
They did not realize that their sins is what your life would cost.
Instead they wanted to live by their own laws,
By adding more words then Moses had written for their cause.
And believing more in their own traditions and not eating bread that was leavened
But they never believed in the one who wrote the laws,
Jesus Christ the son of God sent from heaven.

* * *

    Could you imagine what it would be like if no one believed you were really you? And then, if you were killed simply for refusing to lie about who you are? That's what happened to Jesus. He refused to deny claims to being the Son of God. There are several versions of the song "Son of Heaven." Look up your favorite version today. And, as you reflect on this poem and Luke 23:34, imagine Jesus having so much love for the children of God that he begged the Father to forgive them for their sins as they put him through his torture and death on the cross. That's how much he loves us. People still need prayer for their sins today. Will you pray for them?

34 Then said Jesus, Father, forgive them; for they know not what they do. And they parted his raiment, and cast lots.

(Luke 23:34 KJV)

God's Got the Whole World in His Hands

Why do people think that this world they own?
Why can't people see that this world is God's alone?
That he is the only one that can give or take,
Thinking that we are in control over everything is our biggest mistake.
By not giving our Lord and Savior his credit that is due,
It is our fault for all the headaches and troubles we go through.
Because we do not put our trust in him,
That is why we keep living in disasters that are so grim.
And when we think that this world could not get any worse,
Mankind does something else, and the damage to the world is getting harder to reverse.
But until we study and learn God's word and follow his commands,
Only then will we realize that God is the one who has the whole world in his hands.

* * *

Many of us learned the old hymn "He's Got the Whole World in His Hands" in our youth, but it still stands firm at any age. God's got us—all of us—in his hands. Consider listening to this song as you reflect on 1 Chronicles 29:11. While many of the disasters and damage to the world today are manmade, in the end, God still has the victory because he still reigns on his throne. We need to reach these people who need the love of Christ in their hearts. Who might you share the gospel of Christ with today?

11 Thine, O Lord is the greatness, and the power, and the glory, and the victory, and the majesty: for all that is in the heaven and in the earth is thine; thine is the kingdom, O Lord, and thou art exalted as head above all.

(1 Chronicles 29:11 KJV)

God's Truth and Goodness

God will be there for all people who believe in him,
He favors all people, not just us or them.
He does not care about your color or race,
The Lord shows everyone who believes in him his love, mercy, and grace.
It is up to everyone to open up our hearts, minds, bodies, and souls.
To invite Jesus into our lives and give him complete control.
Because in our lives we will make mistakes and fumble,
But rest assured that God will be right there in our time of trouble.
So, in your life, don't be worried about anything nor be anxious,
Just trust and believe in God's truth and goodness.

* * *

God loves every one of us; he just wants us to open ourselves to him in return. You just have to trust and believe in him to receive his everlasting life. Today, look up the song "Goodness of God" as sung by Tasha Cobbs and think about your relationship with the Lord. As you reflect on this poem and John 6:47, ask yourself if you are holding anything back from Jesus. What do you need to give over to God?

47 Verily, verily, I say unto you, He that believeth on me hath everlasting life.

(John 6:47 KJV)

Everlasting God

Though I walk in this world every day with death so near,
I will continue to put my trust in you, dear Lord, and the sin of death I will no longer fear.
Because I know that you are the one that is in control,
Only in your hands, dear Jesus, my future holds.
So, all my battles will I leave in your hands,
Trusting only in you and not putting my faith in any man.
Because I know that when my enemies come to attack,
I can only look to you, God, to truly have my back.
Because you are my rock, and I find comfort in your holy rod,
You are my rock and salvation; you are my everlasting God.

* * *

The song "Everlasting God," written by Brenton Brown and Ken Riley has since been performed by many artists, but nevertheless inspired this poem. Take a listen to the song today as you reflect on the well-known verse from the Bible, Psalm 23:4. The Lord is always our rock and everlasting salvation in our moment of weakness. Will you put your trust in him today?

4 Yea, though I walk through the valley of the shadow of death, I will fear no evil: for thou art with me; thy rod and thy staff they comfort me.

(Psalm 23:4 KJV)

Jesus Saves

How blessed we are that Jesus loved us and sacrificed his life on a cross,
He did that for us so that our souls would not be at a loss.
Because we can now come to him in our own way,
Confessing to him all our sins that we need to say.
And not feeling guilty, because God wants to forgive,
He does not want us to stay in our sins because he wants us to live.
By being obedient to his laws and commandments that his word covers,
To live a righteous life and to do right by others.
And to live a life of freedom and not being enslaved,
Breaking the bondage of our sins, through his grace, our souls Jesus saves.

* * *

Jesus knew that the soldiers would spit on him and laugh at him, yet he still died for them. He knew we would still sin after knowing about his sacrifice, but he still died for us, too. Today, look up the old hymn "Jesus Saves" as sung by Daryl Coley as you reflect on Romans 5:8. He loves us so much that he pushed through the pain so that we could join him someday in heaven. Have you thanked him today for your freedom?

8 But God commendeth his love toward us, in that, while we were yet sinners, Christ died for us.
   (Romans 5:8 KJV)

In the Name of Jesus

Everything is done through our Lord and Savior,
Jesus is the one that can forgive our sins and offer us his amazing favor.
We should all want to live for Jesus, and through his eyes,
Always spreading his good news with truth and no lies.
By letting the world know that love is what Jesus is all about,
But hate and lies are what the devil wants to continue to put out.
And we must let the world know that Jesus died for our sins,
And happily continue telling the good news that he will be back again.
And when that day arrives, and he comes back for us,
We will give him all the glory and praise, shouting in his name, dear Jesus.

* * *

The best way to put Satan in his place is by shouting the name of Jesus. That's how we, and the Lord, claim victory—every day. Today, look up the old hymn, "In the Name of Jesus" as sung by Theodore Jones and listen to it as you reflect on Mark 16:15. Sharing about Jesus with anyone, even a friend or stranger, is preaching the gospel. Are you preaching the gospel?

15 And he said unto them, Go ye into all the world, and preach the gospel to every creature. (Mark 16:15 KJV)

See You Again

I think about what it must have been like when you came to live among us,
All the people gathering around you, making such a fuss.
Thinking if they could only touch you, their bodies would be healed,
Not knowing that they would be the same people shouting to have you killed.
And even though, Jesus, it was already planned what you had to go through,
You kept right on healing and forgiving us of our sins, and your love for us only grew.
Even though you knew that you would have to suffer and be betrayed,
You stuck around because your truth and your foundation could no longer be delayed.
And you knew that it would take your life, but you went on with your purpose anyway,
Because it was a purpose that you had to fulfill that day.
And even though Satan thought that he had won when your life came to an end,
He did not know, dear Jesus, that you defeated death, and someday he would see you again.

* * *

Satan may have thought that he won when Jesus died on the cross, but three days later, Jesus spoiled Satan's plans, rose again and defeated death. Today, look up Anthony Evans' song "See You Again" and listen to it as you reflect on this poem and Colossians 2:15. Imagine what Jesus went through for us. Knowing where he was going and that he would rise from the dead didn't make it any less painful for him. We should be so thankful for his sacrifice. Have you thanked him today?

15 And having spoiled principalities and powers, he made a shew of them openly, triumphing over them in it. .
    (Colossians 2:15 KJV)

MY FAMILY IN CHRIST (THE WORLD)

Not Believing That Jesus Is Real

People seem to think that they are in complete control,
Not realizing that the power of this world only God truly holds.
And no one can ever measure up to his powers,
He is in control over heaven, earth, storms, hail, and even rain showers.
But we as people, continue to lean on our own understanding,
Not knowing that we are missing out on our blessings for what God has been planning.
But this concept people cannot comprehend,
They prefer to think that there is no God, so they will never have to pay for their sins.
And they believe that they alone are strong and everything they know,
They don't need the Lord's wisdom and knowledge to grow.
And everything is all about them, and this is how they feel,
Not caring about selling their souls to Satan by not believing that Jesus is real.

* * *

Satan spends a lot of time trying to sell his lies that Jesus isn't real. As believers in Christ, we need to pray extra hard for the people who have bought into those lies. And, we need to pray for the right words to say when we come across these people ourselves. Today, look up the song "Too Good to Not Believe" by Cody Carnes and Brandon Lake as you reflect on this poem and John 3:18-20. Remember that Satan hates the light of the world, which is Jesus. Can people see Jesus in you today?

18 He that believeth on him is not condemned: but he that believeth not is condemned already, because he hath not believed in the name of the only begotten Son of God.
19 And this is the condemnation, that light is come into the world, and men loved darkness rather than light, because their deeds were evil.
20 For every one that doeth evil hateth the light, neither cometh to the light, lest his deeds should be reproved.

(John 3:18-20 KJV)

He's Always Right on Time

Sometimes when we are waiting on Jesus,
We may feel that he is in no hurry, don't hear or see us.
But know that he has not forgotten about us when we fall,
And through our faith, he will be there for us when we call.
Just believe that he is working things out for all we do,
He sees our circumstances, and he sees our point of view.
And he knows what is best for us in our life,
We have to continue to put our trust in Jesus and let his will be done,
And his will we should not fight.
Because God will not put us any place we don't belong,
He would never lead us astray or into something wrong.
We get into trouble when we try to go it alone and don't follow God's direction,
But when we are trying to get out of trouble, is when we are crying for his protection.
So, my advice to you is to wait on Jesus and keep this in mind,
His plans for you may not come when you want them to, but he's always right on time.

* * *

If you've ever felt like God has been ignoring you or forgotten about you, you're not alone. Rest assured, he knows what is best for you, and his timing is perfect. He always shows up—right on time! The song "Right on Time" by Aaron Cole (featuring TobyMac) is a great song to look up today. As you reflect on Psalm 27:14, remember to keep your courage as you wait upon the Lord. He will strengthen you, and his plans for you are more than you can imagine for yourself. Will you worship while you wait?

14 Wait on the Lord: be of good courage, and he shall strengthen thine heart: wait, I say, on the Lord.

(Psalm 27:14 KJV)

MY FAMILY IN CHRIST (THE WORLD)

Lord Your Word of Truth Has Always Been Good

God, you are so great,
You can turn a stone heart into love instead of hate,
You can make hearts that are filled with pride,
Fall to their knees and put their selfish ways aside.
Because without you, nothing can be done,
There is no one greater than you dear Lord, no not one,
Even though you cannot be seen,
I will put my trust in your words and what they mean.
Because I know living by your word is all I need,
Living, breathing, and spreading your good news to others, is how I will continue to proceed.
And even though your word to some people may be completely misunderstood,
I know in my life, dear Lord, your word of truth has always been good.

* * *

If you've ever witnessed a real change in someone else's life, you have truly witnessed the power of the Holy Spirit. The Lord can do mighty things in people's lives. Imagine if we all shared the gospel with just one other person, what that would do to this world. It would change the world. Today, look up the song "Your Word Is Truth" by Chris Shalom and listen to it as you reflect on Psalm 147:5. Remember how great the Lord's power is and commit to sharing the gospel with just one person a day. Can you do that today? Together we can change the world.

5 Great is our Lord, and of great power: his understanding is infinite.

(Psalm 147:5 KJV)

God

In the beginning, God created the heavens and the earth,
God also created man, and from man came woman; to mankind she would give birth.
But before God created man and woman, he created day and night,
He created the sky that would bring darkness but also light.
God created the trees, plants, and seeds, which sprouted from this creation of the land,
God did all these things with his mighty hands.
God went on to create fishes, birds, and animals in his own unique way,
How they swam, flew, crawled, or walked was God's final say.
And when God saw all of his creation was good, and his work was done,
He rested on the seventh day because he knew his work on this earth had really just begun.
Because he already knew all the rebellion and disobedience he would come up against,
He knew always what would be in our hearts and minds and the evil intents.
And even though he knew all these things, he still made us in his own image,
It did not stop him from creating a masterpiece in us that he still wants to finish.
But to people who do not believe in him, this concept they can never understand; and to them, this may seem odd,
But to believers like us, we know that he is the forgiving, loving, merciful, wonderful and the one and only God.

* * *

How amazing is it to think that the one who created all the universe and the whole world, looked at his creation and decided the world needed a unique you in this world, too. Even though he knew how this world would end up, he still created us. Today, as you reflect on this poem and Revelation 22:13, look up your favorite worship songs. Create a praise and worship playlist and name it "My Family in Christ (The World), based on this book. Praise the Lord and feel his presence. Can you think of a way to put a little extra kindness into the world today?

13 I am Alpha and Omega, the beginning and the end, the first and the last.

(Revelation 22:13 KJV)

Acknowledgements

I would like to thank my Lord and Savior, Jesus Christ, because without him these religious poems never would have existed. Thank you, Lord, for leading me in the way I should go.

I also would like to thank my husband, Michael G. Norris (a.k.a. Minster Norris G.). Only God knows how much you have supported me every step of the way in all things in my life, and I love you so much, my husband.

I would like to thank my lovely and kindhearted mother, Elouise Abram, who has never turned anyone away that needed help, and who has always supported me in all things.
I would like to thank my sister Sylvia Thompson who has always motivated and encouraged me to do better.

I would like to thank my Grandmother, Lessie B. Ellis, for always being a God-fearing woman and a very strong presence in my life. I love and miss you so much, grandmother.

In loving memory of my Dear sister, Celeste Jones.
In loving memory of my best friend Stephanie Bennett

I would also like to thank Jeannie Culbertson, my sister in Christ—thank you so much for your help in editing my book and for just being so supportive to me on this journey.

And last but certainly not least, I would like to thank Noble Daniel, my brother in Christ—you are the one who brought my book to life with your formatting and your awesome cover design. You both have been such a Godsend from our Lord and Savior, Jesus Christ. Amen!

MY FAMILY IN CHRIST (THE WORLD)

Made in the USA
Middletown, DE
16 March 2023